Praise for
Conversations with Lee Kuan Yew
and the 'Giants of Asia' series

"Thank you for sending me an inscribed copy of *Conversations with Lee Kuan Yew*, which I have been reading with interest and enjoyment. You have done a superb job of capturing the many facets of this extraordinary man, whom I have known and admired for some fifty years. That he is the first to be portrayed in the forthcoming 'Giants of Asia' series seems only right. I appreciate your thinking of me and will look forward to your conversations with the other Giants you propose to include in the series."

Dr Henry A. Kissinger, 56th U.S Secretary of State, 1973–77

"Thank you for your autographed book on *Conversations with Lee Kuan Yew*. It is a fascinating read, even though I am familiar with much of his thoughts and philosophy, having the privilege of working closely under and with him. He is a great teacher, not just for me but also for the younger generations of leaders he brought in."

Goh Chok Tong, former Prime Minister of Singapore, 1990–2004

"Many thanks for sending me your book—*Conversations with Lee Kuan Yew*. I have been a great admirer of Mr Lee ever since I served as former president Chiang Ching-kuo's secretary in the late 80s. I find myself inspired even more today by many of his remarks in your book."

President Ma Ying-jeou, Republic of China (Taiwan)

"There are two types of courage among journalists. Some might risk their lives crossing paths with an IED on an arid back road in Afghanistan. Many fewer risk their reputation by going against the herd of conventional opinion. Tom Plate, America's only syndicated columnist who focuses on Asia, … has taken the second risk in his *Conversations with Lee Kuan Yew*. And it has been a risk well worth taking.… His book could not be more relevant at a moment when recession, debt and dysfunction are plaguing the West while Asia strides boldly into the future.… Much to the credit of Plate's talent, this book reads breezily, despite its heavy themes. It is broken into many easily digestible chapters with titles mimicking movies or television shows.… Overall this was the right choice to make what could easily have been a wonkish drudge into an enjoyable read.… Lee Kuan Yew's wisdom makes sense. Tom Plate has done a fine job of conveying it for a Western audience that ought to be paying attention."

Nathan Gardels, columnist, The Huffington Post

" ...a scintillating insight into the private—and brutally candid—beliefs and thoughts of the 86-year-old Minister Mentor on a wide range of topics, from his temper and children to various countries and his 'authoritarian' ways.... These are captured in a writing style that is fast-paced and conversational over 24 chapters that are peppered with Mr Plate's views...."

Zakir Hussain, The Straits Times (Singapore)

"For veteran American journalist Tom Plate, Minister Mentor Lee Kuan Yew is 'the director of the blockbuster that is Singapore'. The book is written in Mr Plate's trademark humorous, witty and candid style. The conversations in the book cover a wide range of topics. There are serious discussions on philosophy, international relations and governance.... During a break, author and interviewee even banter about what Mr Lee would do if he were to take on the post of United Nations secretary-general. 'I try to get a bit more of [Mr Lee] as a man, as well as a brainiac and as a leader,' said Mr Plate, who also described the politician as 'warm, trusting and open'."

Rachel Chan, TODAY (Singapore)

"Singapore is an economic success story of the modern era, and the man behind this tremendous success is none other than Lee Kuan Yew [who] agreed to give a two-day interview to American journalist Tom Plate.... The author has painted a picture of Lee as a political genius who believes in pragmatism and common sense rather than ideology. Tom Plate's brilliant navigation skills [have produced] many … not-known facets of Yew's leadership and personality."

Dr Ahmed S. Khan, The Dawn (daily newspaper of Pakistan)

"Tom Plate may be one of the few writers able to brag that he once received a note from Lee Kuan Yew saying 'you deserve to be read'. Singapore's senior statesman sent the fax after reading a column Plate had written on China. That might explain why the veteran journalist, who has been writing a weekly syndicated column on America's relationship with Asia since 1996, found it relatively easy to get access to the Minister Mentor for his latest book, *Conversations with Lee Kuan Yew*."

Sonia Kolesnikov-Jessop, The South China Morning Post

"But Plate's "Gee shucks, did they really say that about you?" style has a huge upside. His subjects open up to him in a way they may not have intended to, and the insights the reader gains into their characters are considerable; to the point that Plate's books, for all their faults, will be incomparable for historians, biographers and anyone who ever wants to figure out what made these men, who do deserve to be called 'Giants of Asia', tick.

Sholto Byrnes, The National (Abu Dhabi)

GIANTS *of* ASIA

conversations with

LEE KUAN YEW

CITIZEN SINGAPORE:
HOW TO BUILD
A NATION

SPECIAL EDITION

TOM PLATE

Marshall Cavendish
Editions

Conversations with Lee Kuan Yew was first published in 2010.
Second edition published 2013.

This third edition published 2015 by Marshall Cavendish Editions
An imprint of Marshall Cavendish International, 1 New Industrial Road, Singapore 536196

Photographs courtesy of Yeong Yoon Ying / Research by My Lu
Design by Bernard Go Kwang Meng / Cover illustration by P. K. Cheng
Project editor: Lee Mei Lin

Other Marshall Cavendish Offices
Marshall Cavendish Corporation. 99 White Plains Road, Tarrytown NY 10591-9001, USA •
Marshall Cavendish International (Thailand) Co Ltd. 253 Asoke, 12th Flr, Sukhumvit 21 Road,
Klongtoey Nua, Wattana, Bangkok 10110, Thailand • Marshall Cavendish (Malaysia) Sdn Bhd,
Times Subang, Lot 46, Subang Hi-Tech Industrial Park, Batu Tiga, 40000 Shah Alam, Selangor
Darul Ehsan, Malaysia.

Marshall Cavendish is a trademark of Times Publishing Limited

National Library Board Singapore Cataloguing in Publication Data
Plate, Tom, author.
Conversations with Lee Kuan Yew : citizen Singapore : how to build a nation / Tom Plate. – Third
edition – Singapore : Marshall Cavendish Editions, 2015.
pages cm. - (Giants of Asia)
"Special edition."
Includes bibliographical references.
ISBN : 978-981-4677-61-5 (hardcover)

Lee, Kuan Yew, 1923-2015 - Interviews. 2. Lee, Kuan Yew, 1923-2015 – Political and social views.
3. Prime ministers – Singapore - Interviews. I. Title. II. Series: Giants of Asia.

DS610.73.L45
959.5705092 -- dc23   OCN910538878

Printed in Singapore by Markono Print Media Pte Ltd

Asked what they thought about **Lee Kuan Yew** and his legacy, here are what these world figures and experts had to say.

"Lee Kuan Yew can justifiably be called the Father of Modern Singapore. He has steered through policies that have been copied across Asia, and have greatly lifted the profile and representation of Singapore. It is a legacy that will endure."

John Major, Prime Minister of Britain, 1990–97

"He is a big frog in a small pond. He is not satisfied with what he has. He had ambitions to become Prime Minister of all Malaysia. He tries to lecture people but people dislike that. People do regard him as an intellectual, as something more than just an ordinary politician. He's always invited to give his views on things and, to that extent, he is something bigger than Singapore. But the fact remains that he is [only] the Mayor of Singapore. This is something he doesn't like. You see, he wants to be big. And he feels that we [in Malaysia] took away his opportunity to lead a real country. But I think he will go down in history as a very remarkable intellectual and politician at the same time, which is not a very often thing."

Dr Mahathir bin Mohamad,
Prime Minister of Malaysia, 1981–2003

"Is a leader the product of his times, or does a leader make his times? Lee Kuan Yew is a living testimony to the truth of both assertions: the birth of a new nation-state—Singapore—was the unique moment in time which drove this man to rise to the call of history; and in his single-minded resolve to wrestle his city-state from the Third World into the First, he shaped his times, creating the Singapore way of development, which some look up to, and some decry. It is a fact, however, that if two names could be indissociable, these would be Singapore & LKY, and LKY & Singapore."

Ton Nu Thi Ninh, former Vietnamese Ambassador to the
European Union, and founder of Tri Viet University, Vietnam

"President and Mrs. Carter's full agenda makes it impossible for them to respond positively to the many requests to contribute to books."

Jimmy Carter, U.S. President, 1977–81.
Currently President of the Carter Foundation
(signed by some spokesperson, not by any of the Carters)

"The Queen has asked me to thank you for your letter. Her Majesty was interested to read about your literary project entitled Giants of Asia, and has taken careful note of your request. I am afraid, however, that throughout her reign The Queen has made it a rule not to publicly express her personal views. I am sorry to send you a disappointing reply, but may I send my good wishes for the success of your project. Yours sincerely, Mrs. Sonia Bonici."

Buckingham Palace, London, on behalf of HRH Queen Elizabeth II

"It has often been said that today, the natural resources that a society has in hand are not as important as the knowledge and the strategy of its human resources. Singapore is an excellent example of this and LKY has made it so. It is not a miracle that transformed Singapore from being a small and poor 'phone booth' size sleeping community, into one of the world's most impressive success stories; it was Lee Kuan Yew. Whether one agrees or disagrees with him, his success is on record. He is an intellectual and a statesman, one with a vision, one with a strategy and the ability to get things done. Readers will have much to learn from his story."

Kantathi Suphamongkon, 39th Thai Foreign Minister.
Currently Visiting Professor of Law and Diplomacy at the
University of California, Los Angeles (UCLA), and Senior Fellow
at the Burkle Center for International Relations, UCLA

"Singapore is a city-state that had poor odds for surviving, let alone thriving: no resources, tiny size and population, and surrounded by difficult and sometimes hostile neighbors. Through sheer intellect and willpower, LKY carved out a country that is a model for economic growth, has little or no corruption, is a visionary in digital technology and delivers a first-rate education and life for its citizens."

Professor Jeffrey Cole, Director of the Center for the Digital Future,
University of Southern California (USC)

"No one has ever done state-guided capitalism better. If China can model itself on Singapore, the world will be a much better place. Education, health care, social investment, individual incentive, reasonable attention to the environment—a good balance. He created stability in the region—an amazingly high degree of leverage, primarily by commercial/economic example. Also the smart use of military capability, never apparently applied, which is the best sort of military force. Look after things well at home, and have a strong arm, and you can influence others. I hope that he feels very good about what he's done. Regarding the issue of alleged excessive social control: it's sort of like banking and finance—the right level of regulation has a lot of sense to it."

Wyatt (Rory) Hume, Director, Education, Training and Development for the Research Division of the Qatar Foundation; Provost, United Arab Emirates University; and former Provost, University of California system

"Lee Kuan Yew has made Singapore absolutely unique in this part of the world, by making it as one of the least corrupt political systems in the world.... Now that is a tremendous achievement. The question is, how long can you maintain an incorrupt political system?" (stated publicly in 2000)

Samuel Huntington, 1927–2008, author of The Clash of Civilizations and the Remaking of World Order

Contents

Day Two

Preface:
The Lion in Winter

SPENDING AN AFTERNOON with an American journalist would not exactly be anyone's idea of a rollicking great time. So I was a little surprised when he agreed to sit for this book. I figured my chances at no better than 50-50. Then again, Lee Kuan Yew was not one to duck an important part of his job and certainly no mere journalist from any country would fluster him.

So when he said yes, I knew it was because he would want to advance the Singapore story as he wished outsiders to understand it, and he knew I would be a good listener. After all, I had proposed a book in which he would do a lot of the talking.

And he knew me a little. The back-story was that in 1996, the first year of my newspaper column in the *Los Angeles Times* on Asia and America, the then-titled Senior Minister (and without a doubt, still the power) had agreed to a one-on-one interview.

From that session, Lee's clear views helped me understand that, to a large extent, the future of Asia might be shaped by the contours of the China-U.S. relationship more than any other factor. Again, it has to be emphasized that this is back in 1996, when China was not yet the obsession of the Western media.

At that first session in his office at the Istana, I remember him greeting me in his trademark button-front cardigan, then quickly seating himself in his comfort chair—but tentatively, almost as if not planning to stay long. A practiced wariness searched my face, as if readying for the inevitable volley of caning and chewing gum queries (then the main interest of U.S. journalism) that would start his clock ticking toward interview closure.

He got neither caning nor chewing gum baloney from me. I wasn't interested in re-hearing what I already knew from re-reading old U.S. media stories; I wanted to know what he knew that I didn't know. The interview lasted longer than scheduled. And it was the first of several that helped pave the way for the book-length conversation sessions of the summer of 2009. So it is fair to say that from all this, he knew more or less what to expect from me when we embarked upon this book 13 years later. I knew he could not always agree with the views of someone from Los Angeles, where I was based at my university, but on occasion you might hear something or other from him. Once he faxed a copy of one of my columns with the scribbled encouragement that my views on China "deserve to be read". It would be dishonest not to tell you that this encouragement was appreciated. And I was hardly the only American over the decades to accept his tutoring. Whatever his faults and mistakes, and he made his share, he helped many of us in the West understand the political mystery and growing importance of Asia better, and in the process perhaps understand ourselves and our own assumptions better too.

So in the beginning of the 2009 sessions for this book, I was surprised when he seemed a little nervous. During an early break, when he went somewhere for a few minutes, I managed to catch the ear of Lee's hovering press secretary to ask her, in effect, why the lion in winter seemed so edgy. Madam Yeong Yoon Ying was her name, and bluntness was her game. This formidable lady's style could scare the Singapore media half to death, but Americans are okay with bluntness and so we got along rather nicely. And indeed she did not agonize over the question but looked at me straight and said, as if the answer were insanely obvious: "…because he's worried about what you will write!"

It had not occurred to me that anything from a Western journalist would matter much one way or the other to Lee Kuan Yew. But in the winter of one's life, perhaps things either matter not at all—or then they matter very much. And for Lee, the outside image of Singapore did mean a great deal. Years before, I had asked him why he bothered to see me when I was in town. He looked at me as if I were joking, then answered: "Because I want to influence the people who influence other people." And so for Lee Kuan Yew any book about him that was sympathetic, however defined or even marginally so, would be a favorable snapshot of Singapore. He did not see a big difference between himself and his country.

And, for most of his half century at the top of Singapore, neither did many outsiders.

He was 87 when he surprised a lot of people and made an appearance at the official book launch of *Conversations with*

Lee Kuan Yew. This was in May 2010 at the Shangri-La Hotel. I was told that he had never graced a book party before, but had finally agreed, just a few days prior. I met his car at the VIP side entrance of the hotel and when he finally managed to get himself out and steady himself, I asked how it was going.

"I'm degrading rapidly, Tom," he said, and he shuffled forward into the hotel step by step. I did not say anything.

Aides warned me with particular authoritative ferocity—after telling me repeatedly that he would not show at all—that on the off chance that he actually made the party, he would not be saying anything at the event. He entered the reception room and sat down in a chair in a line of others arrayed in front of the small podium. After a bit of ceremony and a run through several speakers, the last being myself, he stared at me and said, "Can I say something?"

What do aides ever know, right?

I said of course and ushered him to the podium.

As it turned out, he did not say much but what he said made me happy. Clearing his throat, and standing erect at the podium, he said: "I don't agree with all of it, but that is to be expected ... the Western journalist's exaggeration of eccentricity. But on the whole, he got my point of view across." That was good enough for me.

In retrospect, five years later, and just a handful of weeks after his death in hospital at the age of 91, on March 23, this comment seems considerably more than good enough. This unusual man was as demanding of the journalist as he was of himself—and of his colleagues and of his Singapore. There was no mediocrity about or in him. You knew that in the first few minutes of meeting him. You had better be on your game.

It is true that I have not ever lived in Singapore. I have been a child of New York and an adult of Los Angeles. It is difficult to estimate the overlap of these three very different urban cultures. But surely, while it is much less than 100 percent, it is also much more than zero. The bottom line is we all live on the same planet, facing the same huge common problems, whether citizens of Bangladesh or Boston, Singapore or Spain.

Lee Kuan Yew was not my president or my dean or my father-in-law. But he was one of the most important tutors in my life. I learned a great deal from our conversations and interviews. Almost all of them are memorable. Almost all of them are now included this book, which in effect represents its third edition. To me they form a powerful totality of thought and approach, as well as a panoramic portrait of a restless and relentless pragmatist: Let's figure it out, let's get it done, let's stop fooling around or fooling ourselves that the problems are just going to vanish on their own. Put the best minds on it, don't be lazy, work harder.

This positive attitude was one of the many things I found endearing and valuable about him. And so this is the one book I wrote about him. Whatever its inadequacies, at least it did 'get his views across'. We need to learn from them. He had a lot to say to us. What follows is some of that.

Tom Plate, Beverly Hills, June 2015

conversations with

LEE
KUAN
YEW

Introduction

The following conversation took place out of range of the four open tape recorders that account for all the many direct quotes attributed to Lee Kuan Yew throughout this book. This informal exchange took place in the middle of the second day, out on the terrace of Istana Negara Singapura—Istana for short. It is put here for a reason that explains itself.

WITH A LITTLE bit of body English, Lee Kuan Yew, the hard-nosed founder of modern Singapore, motions to me that it is time for a break in all the talk. This means—and there's no arguing with this gent and certainly not on his home territory!—that it is time for a break. Period!

So we raise ourselves up from the table set for us at a far end of the State Room by what looks like a fireplace (but how could such exist in ever-sweltering Singapore?), but in fact is an odd little lonely raised stage with curtains. We straggle through a large door that leads to a long shade-dulled exterior corridor and then move out onto a broad and sun-scorched plaza a few careful steps of marble below. It overlooks the well-named Function Lawn, Gun Terrace and Edinburgh Road that leads to Orchard Road, the country's main retail thoroughfare. Visible in the near distance is the dramatic, busting-out-all-over downtown Singapore skyline.

No more than 5'10" (1.78 m) tall, but trim of figure, and yet laboring through his mid-eighties step by step, he rubs one weary hand over his pale forehead and coal-black eyes as we lose the protective shade of the cool State Room and accept a plunge into the burning furnace of late-afternoon equatorial Singapore.

The temperature is about 90° F (32° C), and the humidity is at about 90 percent; and so we are moving very cautiously, unwilling to confront the next blanket of discomfort in any bold fashion. Then, suddenly, at about the same time, we start joking with one another. Out of nowhere erupts this silly flurry of light-hearted badinage. This comes after hours of conversation ranging from the political deficiencies of today's democracies to the sustaining qualities of meditation to the dynamics of relating to the rise of China.

Not many people know how witty this thoroughly modern Machiavellian Master can be. I start joking about the United Nations, and he banters back like he is guest-host of a political comedy show. We go at it for a few minutes (see the story "Time for a Break" on pages 209–214), but then the mood changes again, as if an unexpected waft of breeze had blown in from across the Strait.

Turning back toward the State Room to finish up the final hour of discussion, he stops suddenly, hit with what almost seems like a little fear. He stares into my eyes for a few seconds, then looks off and focuses on a distant white Doric column. There is something he wants to say, but doesn't know how quite to put it. He doesn't want to insult me, but he wants this particular stone, or pebble, uncovered.

It is a rare moment of pause for this supremely articulate and self-confident man. I wait. I will not put words in his mouth for him.

Finally, he blinks a few flutters, pivots 90 degrees to turn to me and face me frontally—almost blocking me with his body—and whispers, point-blank, in that perfect British diction that the first time you hear it knocks you off your chair, something like this to me: 'Tom, the book will have to have critical and negative stuff in it. I know, don't worry about me. Just write me up exactly as you see me. Let the chips fall where they may. Tell the true story of me, as you see it. That's all I ask.' Then he nods for us to proceed apace.

Before we walk on, back to the State Room, I nod to assure him that this indeed is the plan.

But the truth is that his unexpected comment worries me in a way that would bother few Western journalists. The 'warts' in the Lee Kuan Yew story are just not that interesting to me; the negatives are well known, and it's the story that over the decades he has most often read about himself, especially in the Western media: the steely willpower, the dismissive if not obnoxious attitude toward critics, the mean Machiavellian maneuvering around weak opponents and grinding them to dust, the haughty soft authoritarianism.

But this is not the Lee Kuan Yew I know and find most interesting, nor the one I want to tell you about. For when I first met him in 1996, I was astonished by the range of his interests and the depth of his insights. I spent the rest of the day trying to think of someone I had interviewed who was like him. There wasn't anyone. And over the decades I've been lucky to interview many world leaders and leading thinkers.

For my column about Asia, launched in the *Los Angeles Times* in 1995 and still rolling on via worldwide syndication in other newspapers (from Dubai to Providence in Rhode Island), I interviewed him four times between 1996 and 2007. This book is based primarily on a pair of quite lengthy and arduous exclusive interviews in Singapore in the summer of 2009 that aim to capture the brainpower and the range of the man.

So this is not a book about how most in the Western media view the controversial founder of modern Singapore. It is, however, an honest and full account of the Lee Kuan Yew I know. I hope it is heavy on insight and feeling; I know it is low on 'warts'. I don't know whether Lee Kuan Yew will be disappointed about that; I certainly hope you won't be.

Prologue to the
Interviews at the Istana

IT IS 4 P.M.—the maddening mid-afternoon sauna of a sizzling Singapore summer. And it's raining like Sumatra, with aluminum siding sheets of water sliding down from the sky.

I duck into the hotel car for the short drive to the Istana, which in the Malay language means 'palace', for the first two-hour session with Lee Kuan Yew. Tooling along exactly at the posted speed limit—no more, no less—the driver navigates steadily down Orchard Road, the glitzy shopping thoroughfare. My mind should have been doting on economic statistics, political philosophy, Chinese history and other such fine stuff. For months I have been boning up for this and I was as ready as I would ever be. But weirdly, the heat or the occasion or whatever must have gotten to me because I am off in some mad mind-sphere, imagining LKY as some mysterious mogul in the American movie business—as a famous Hollywood figure, in fact.

Outsiders sometimes diminish Singapore by suggesting it is no more than a nation-as-corporation and dubbing it 'Singapore Inc'. What a misreading! No corporation in the history of the world was ever as interesting and complex as this place.

Unsurprisingly, Singaporeans tend to get riled by the Inc. moniker. I get irked by it, too, and I don't even live here. I just hope my Singapore friends don't get as irritated by my own Hollywood style analogy. It's not Singapore as a bland corporation, but Singapore as a spectacular dramatic epic movie.

For worse or for better, I live and work in Southern California, in the vast sprawling suburb that includes the independent city of Beverly Hills where famous Hollywood people live—and then me. Here, people hunker down and mentally imagine the world as one big blockbuster movie or another.

Here in what we sometimes call 'Hollyweird', no reality is more real than the bottom-line figures of the Box Office take. The movie *Titanic* is a perfect example. Normal people knew it as a very familiar story of an historic cruise ship going down. But denizens of Hollywood, before opening day, saw it as a metaphor for a production company that would sink in a sea of red ink even faster than the real Titanic. They didn't think it would float; they thought it would drop like a rock to the bottom of the sea. They were quite wrong.

And so it is with Singapore, imagined as a movie. Here is a story about a little island country that, perhaps until relatively recently, few had heard of—except perhaps about some nonsense or other concerning chewing gum and caning. Who cares? How can it succeed? What's the hook?

Decades later, Singapore is one roaring success. It's practically a classic. The bottom-line figures are as green as the carefully organized landscaping, and the place has an airport like a movie set and an infrastructure the envy of Dubai; it has home ownership for 95 percent of the citizens, shopping malls out of *Beverly Hills 90210*, public schools that put America's to shame, international science and math scores even higher than Japan's, and a national airline that reminds its passengers that flying needn't be cruel and unusual punishment. What's most telling is that giant countries, especially China, sometimes India, and now even fast-growing Vietnam, wonder how Singapore made it so big and so quickly. They want to learn Singapore's secrets. Right, no one wants to imitate a failure. So if imitation is the sincerest form of flattery, Singapore today is one of the more flattered countries in the world.

Lee Kuan Yew, modern Singapore's legendary founder, and his beloved country are interchangeable. Ton Nu Thi Ninh, that elegant lady from nearby Vietnam, puts this so well in the front of the book: "It is a fact ... that if two names could be indissociable, these would be Singapore & LKY, and LKY & Singapore."

That's a nice high-level sentiment, but I am from crass Hollywood/Beverly Hills. So I am looking for something less intellectual, more like ... gross bottom line! So I imagine Lee as a famous movie director. You can just see him sitting on the set in the Director's Chair, barking out orders with his crisp, decisive, can-do autocratic style, his jutting jaw and drop-dead look. Go ahead, you wishy-washy liberals—*Make My Day*.

That profile is so beloved here in Hollywood. Knee-jerk ultra-liberals though many are, many here are also bottom-line studio executives and time-pressed stars and starlets alike. Don't-give-a-darn decisiveness goes over big time in this town. Lee is like an autocratic Alfred Hitchcock folded into the trim figure of Ang Lee.

And by far—we imagine—LKY's most famous film would in fact be 'Singapore'. We imagine his masterpiece in the grand tradition of *Gone With The Wind*. It is a tale of how one man's honest team of founding fathers sweep into power after the collapse of the brutal occupying Japanese (normal casting: almost always the bad guys in Hollywood films), fight off alien communists (as well as corrupting Western values), marry Malaysia and then divorce her after just a few years (typical Hollywood, right?)—see "Trouble in Paradise" on pages 164–174—and then with Machiavellian acumen manage to outwit the Western multinational corporations seeking to exploit the country and its hardworking people. The movie ends with sweeping pans of the bursting skyline and well-manicured parks and immaculate homes of this Asian neo-utopia, the richest country in the region and, perhaps, its most envied.

And it takes LKY and his team less than a generation to do this. What a story! And what a commercial success! So, should we get Lee ready for the ritual pounce up onto the Oscar Stage to pick up his Lifetime Achievement Award and to thank everyone in his extended Chinese family?

In truth, the controversy over this 'Singapore' blockbuster is not quite settled legend yet. The place somehow remains a perpetual puzzle. Who knows where Lee will wind up in the firmament of greats! But one thing is certain: there's never been a production number quite like Singapore.

So this is the story of what it's like to spend a few hours in deep conversation with this iconic and fashionably authoritarian director.

It's a story that needs to be told. Many people, mainly those who have never visited, think his Singapore is some sort of tortured totalitarian Martian planet out of Aldous Huxley's novel *Brave New World*—the sort of never-never land where that which isn't prohibited, is mandated. And in some limited sense they are right. But just go there and visit, and you'll see they are also quite wrong.

Your first time, you think there is something surreal about it all. The feeling (it's not creepy, just palpably different) hits you minutes after you land. The airport is a knockout and the sense of not being on this planet proceeds apace on the drive from the airport to your hotel.

You glance out a car window. The scene is not quite right. Something is missing. It bothers you, but what bothers you worse is you can't put your finger on it. And you think maybe it should hit you right in the face.

But then you get it—it's what's NOT visible. There are no McDonald's bags, no KFC containers, no abandoned cars, no dead bodies (only slight joke, I was raised in the New York/New Jersey area), no homeless camps, no in-your-face beggars (where are they?

they have to be somewhere!). It's absolutely, totally, amazingly, and unbelievably … clean!

This is a city? It's not any place I've seen, you say…

The same feeling hits you downtown where, you discover, women claim they can walk the streets any hour of the night without hassle, much less assault. Drug gangs don't monopolize the parks and intimidate moms, strollers and families that are hoping for nothing more than some urban peace. Again, where's the street-side littering, the homeless mini-cities, the screaming traffic horns? Green trees and flora everywhere, and the air—even the air feels clean.

You don't see that much laundry hanging out on the terraces, as in many parts of Asia. You can sit down at a café and put your hand under the table, and never come in contact with a 'pre-owned' piece of gum left behind as if a deliberate irritant. Call this the poisoned fruit of authoritarian rule, if you will; I call it sane and sanitary, and I'm for more of it!

Also notably missing at times are the feral traffic snarls (like in notorious Cairo) or the endless cascades of dirty concrete jungle (like in the city-state of New York) or the teeming masses out in the open whose zip codes stand for little more than one big forlorn shantytown. *Oh Calcutta!*

Not here.

But there are other things you might genuinely miss, though it may take a few days to sort it all out in your head—and this is the other side of paradise. You might truly miss vigorous criticism of the central government in the news media, or the kind of British-style parliamentary debate that stands your hair on end. You can go to the gorgeous parks but perhaps miss the anti-establishment political orators, the cup-open itinerant musician, the oddball scene of any kind. What's more, you may miss the drama of jury trials; they don't have them here—and they are proud of having qualified judges making the call. You may also be offended by the policy of capital punishment for drug dealers (again, without peer jury—the judge *is* the jury).

On the other hand, you'll be happy about the relative absence of corruption (even police are paid as well as other government civil servants, which is well above the Western average), admire the low infant mortality rates (Singapore's health record leads most countries in almost all health categories), and appreciate the gun policy (no one has them except the police).

But, then again, back to the other hand ... you might really miss the atmosphere of vigorous open criticism of the city-state's leaders. There isn't any to speak of. Don't you dare disrespectfully criticize, for this is Singapore, and since the 1950s, it has been run by one man (and the elite around him). His full name is Harry Lee Kuan Yew, but Harry is used rarely, maybe by close friends, or enemies who needle that he's more British than Chinese. Anyway, LKY, at this writing, is now 86 years of age. It's past time you met him.

DAY ONE

One Late Afternoon
in the Summer of 2009

HE WALKS IN and slips me a nod, now closing in at about 15 feet away. But he lacks his chipper little step of yore.

LKY, it appears, has a cold.

We shake hands. I notice immediately that his office did pass along my request that we dress very casually (and that these sessions take place anywhere but in the formality of his office). I suppress a chuckle. This grungy level of casual I hadn't quite expected. Here is this precise and even elegant statesman decked out in nondescript neo-warehouse clothes, shrouded in the trademark windbreaker, with workman's trousers and some kind of generic slippers. The whole outfit seems as suited for a man about to clean out his garage as undergo the ordeal of questioning by a Western journalist!

Then you see the distress of pain. His stoic face has a look of weary persecution and his walk is a sort of gravity-challenging, leaning-forward step-by-step-without-falling mini-jog. This is from a vigorous man who has spent an adult lifetime in serious worship of an exercise machine. He does not favor the impediments of cold or injury. He coughs and this seems impossible. Since 1996 I've interviewed him three times. His first remark to me was always: "Tom, get on the treadmill, lose some weight."

He was right—as is often the case.

For decades he has developed his brain as a mix of British positivism, classic Chinese Sun Tzu strategizing, and flat-out Singaporean nationalism. That brain has been honed and shaped inside a well-toned, healthy body made in Sparta-via-Singapore. Philosophers have often written of the 'mind-body' problem. But with LKY there has been no problem; it all seems to fit like a Singapore-made Swiss clock that just keeps on ticking.

But when he is obviously low like this, you almost joke: Singapore is such a small country, the place might well come to a stop if the founder were to slow down; everyone might just as well take the day off and stay in bed.

Of course, you remind yourself, he is no longer prime minister (his son is); of course he is off-to-the-side and well off the pitch (doubtful), and all of that. But as long as this legendary statesman is alive, he is to Singapore what the center is to a circle—in the middle of the whole deal.

And now he has a cold!

Seriously, I feel sorry for him, having never felt this from him before. They say LKY is a clammy methodical fish, but I never have found him that way. To people close to him and around him, he has been meticulous, demanding, impatient and, yes, sometimes brutally dismissive. But with me, at least, he has been a helpful and patient tutor in the all-important subjects of politics, governance and international relations. He is passionate about ideas (especially when they work or make sense), about Singapore's uniqueness (as long as you don't make fun of it, especially the chewing gum and caning part), about not tolerating political stupidity (unless it's from the U.S. Congress—a rich source—and then he'll try so hard to keep his mouth shut), about imbecility in governance (never—he hopes—his own), and about asserting an essential role for Asia on the world stage (dominated in recent centuries by the Americans and the Europeans, but perhaps this century, eventually, by Asia).

His own superiority complex arises in part from his sense of what's required to help redress Asia's long-suffering inferiority complex.

Lee, now titled 'Minister Mentor' (not my all-time favorite title for a serious official position!), and I are seated round a dining table, in the far corner of a very large room. It is called the State Room, and it is much larger than the Oval Office of the White House, though not in the same league as the Delegates' Lounge off to the side of the General Assembly at the United Nations in New York. But it is in a league of its own as a reminder of the legacy of British colonialism. You could imagine Winston Churchill calling in his war cabinet, lighting a cigar, sitting down in one of the large yellow sofas and feeling right at home. That is, until he ventured outside—and got hit in the face by the climatic oven of the equator. Sunny Singapore, oh yes, is no gray London.

But in the afternoon, you might want to stay cool and remain inside, as we are right now: Lee Kuan Yew and myself, with two of his aides, in this gorgeous, chandeliered, cavernous room that is air-conditioned as severely as a warehouse of perishables.

So it is cool and slightly dark in the corner where we are, sectioned off to create a feeling of intimacy by a wide Chinese partition, mostly dark emerald and decorated elegantly with birds and flowers. It is easy on the eyes. Over against a panel of old-style rectangular floor-to-ceiling windows that overlook the connecting corridor, a pair of physical rehab aides (he has his own physiotherapy team) stand still as statuettes, waiting to replenish the heat pad on the battered right leg of the ordinarily fit-to-a-tee statesman.

LKY turns his head a little to the left and looks at me as if to say, let's get going. He keeps tightening the thigh-warming pad and looking over to a male physical therapist in white who will keep running in with ones freshly warmed. An injury suffered while dismounting an exercise bike (a daily ritual) has suddenly turned this otherwise physically vigorous former head-of-government into something more like an old man finally looking his age.

To lighten the atmosphere I try to ease into my Cool-Complimentary-Mode. I float out a silly comment—something along the lines of how well the recent trek to neighboring Malaysia went. It doesn't work, it seems off-key, and I should have known better. This much-celebrated and much-criticized guru of modern successful Singapore, this high priest of traditional Asian/Confucian values, this bête noire of Western human rights groups, this hard-nosed exponent of what Westerners have termed 'soft authoritarianism', this formidable intellect—is not one for gratuitous brown-nosing. Even as he plows on deep into the eighth decade of his life, he gives you the feeling that he is a man in a hurry, wherever it is he is still going. Generally, flattery gets you nowhere: it's as if he feels such fluff only slows him down, distracts him from seeing the end point, and perhaps even is aimed at lulling him into some kind of rhetorical ambush.

He glances back at me with eyes that usually seem to hide so much—because they have seen so much over the decades—but this time convey only the slightest of irritation. Yes, there's a fearsome side to LKY, and he is not exactly a role model for everyone. He is always knocked about by human rights organizations of the West for Singapore's near-automatic death-to-drug-dealers policy and general stern sentencing policies. Few Westerners find charming his wily ways of manhandling serious political opponents. Scores tend to be settled in the courts, where, almost miraculously, LKY never loses a case, and the inevitable losers find themselves plunged into financial doom. Outsiders have described this approach as a 'soft authoritarian' style of governance.

For many Westerners, in fact, Singapore is little more than a technologically psyched-up, soft-core gulag of caning, don't walk on the grass (and don't smoke any grass), no chewing gum allowed, don't do anything unless we tell you it's not specifically prohibited, and be careful if you openly criticize the founder of modern Singapore because the inherited and still-used British anti-defamation laws tilt toward representatives of the state.

So all I am expressing to LKY as we start is my hope that this little book of our conversations will attract enough curiosity in the West to take us all beyond clichés and half truths, prompting us all to begin thinking out of the conventional political box. We in the West might even wind up appreciating Singapore for what it is—triumphs, warts, whatever.

For just a second, the old cocky and defiant LKY surfaces amid the coughs and sighs and pangs of pain. His face, though well lined, is animated; he is grinning now, so very alert: "Well, I think what the Western world readership does not understand is that at the end of the day, I am not worried by how they judge me. I am worried by how the people I have governed judge me. I owe them this responsibility when I put myself up for election in the 50s, won it, took them into Malaysia and took them out of Malaysia. We had to make an independent Singapore work."

He is suddenly on his first roll; there will be many today and tomorrow. He is a master explainer and convincer, so watch out! He's hard to resist! He continues: "It was an enormous burden I thought I could not discharge. We had to create a new economy. But I had a good team. Empirically, we tried one approach after the other and finally succeeded. After succeeding, my next job [he resigned as PM in 1990] was to find successors who would carry on the system because if it breaks down, then all that I have done will come to naught.

"So, I had a successor in [former PM] Goh Chok Tong [now senior minister] and a team with him. I stayed behind to show him how he can change things. If he wants to change this, this is the way to do it. No crushing of gears. Within six months, three ministers left because they didn't like his style. I talked them out of it. I said, give him time, he needs to settle in. They stayed on and he carried on for 14 years. I helped him. He appointed my son deputy who helped him succeed.

"Goh's success means I have succeeded, not that he has succeeded only. His success reflects creditably on me. He has decided to help my son [Lee Hsien Loong] succeed because that will reflect favorably on him. We have evolved a system, a virtual cycle. At some point, it may break down because the ablest and the brightest may not come in to do the job because they think all is well, why should they expose themselves to press publicity, constrict their family life? If that happens, we will have an alternative government."

I slip a word in: "But you are pretty proud of what you have?" I do not dredge up the well-known Singapore jibe that the triumphant triad is sometimes labeled as 'the Father, the Son and the Holy Goh'.

"It was the best that I could do with the people that I had."

I explain that this is the story—the amazing 'Singapore' movie—that needs to hit America's movie screens. We in the West need to know more about this place, rejecting what is not right for America but keeping our minds open to borrowing and adapting what might still work for us.

He shakes his head—slowly, with a little fatigue—then tightens the warming pad around his right thigh, sips a bit of water from a small glass on the card table put in front of us, and tells me that he doesn't think much of that possibility.

"No," he replies in his characteristic pessimist-realist tone, with that overlay of British accent that fogs over centuries of Chinese heritage. "Only those interested in international affairs and in East Asia will bother, no matter what you do. The average American only knows Singapore as some faraway place, unless they have visited it. If they did, they would have been surprised that it was not the sort of place they expected!"

Cued by the boss, a rehab aide jets toward the senior statesman with another heat pad. LKY tightens it almost fiercely, as if only a painful vice-like grip will expunge the pain.

I look at him: "You're right, dismay might attend modern Singapore's failure to live up to the old cliché."

He nods: "They don't know where Singapore is, they are not interested. They think of only Michael Fay [the infamous graffiti teen delinquent who in 1994 went on a spray painting spree in Singapore and was thus caned], then maybe caning, chewing gum … strange odd place this Singapore."

For too long a time, the issue of banned chewing gum (now largely legally chewable) clouded up Western media lenses whenever they focused on this island city-state. Reports spun chewing gum into a metaphor for Singapore's peculiar ways, and/or for its lock-step, police-state proclivities. For many years as a visiting columnist, I too chewed over the puzzle of the chewing gum conundrum, but came to understand that the tendency to stick the remains of the gum in every which place was viewed by the authorities as a palpable attack on Singapore's ambition to be perfect. That is, it was anti-utopian. It was gumming up the works. As far as LKY and his team were concerned, the yucky habit, commonplace in the old days, was a palpable enemy of progress. The way to edge forward toward utopia was simple: simply outlaw chewing gum.

> ...what the Western world readership does not understand is that at the end of the day, I am not worried by how they judge me. I am worried by how the people I have governed judge me.

But hasn't the Western media moved beyond the chewing gum nonsense, all the same? Surely these past impressions have been overtaken by enlightened new perspectives on Singapore?

Lee, fiddling with the latest heat pad as he replies, looks at me and then down at his right leg: "I am not sure we are past history. But the media have stopped flogging the dead horse. They can see that there is a different Singapore. It is no longer sterile, it's no longer an absence of fun."

He starts to warm up here, as if looking both backwards and forwards: "We have put on a colorful gloss and buzz. For high culture, we have many museums, art galleries, rap and whatever else they are doing in the discos, beer and wine-drinking by the riverside. They boost the tourist trade. It is part of a world culture."

The Clarke Quay waterfront span near Singapore's downtown area is a major tourist attraction. Somehow—you have to chuckle—it's very hard to imagine LKY leaning against a bar in the wee hours watching the street action and running up a tab.

I try once again—one last time. I explain that the challenge in writing this book is to reach people who are unaware of the change, and who he really is, and so I add: "I want to get to that interior LKY. I don't have to convince Singaporeans that you are important, and I don't have to convince even the neighboring Malaysians that you are important, or perhaps anyone in this region of this."

Lee, coughing heavily (he's a non-smoker), starts to interrupt, but I am determined to finish my point and plunge on: "But if I do this book right, it could be a great help to Americans trying to understand what you stand for. Look, people in Singapore know you are an important man but..."

He stops me in my tracks with a bit of negative body language. Referring to my comment about how well Singaporeans know him, he hits me with this: "They think they know me, but they only know the public me."

It seems we have hit a nerve.

Father Knows Best

Born and raised on the island of Singapore, living here all his life except for schooling abroad and a lot of hard-driving globe-trotting, LKY has held the center of the island city-state's public life for more than five decades. And he thinks even Singaporeans don't really know him—much less outsiders? Amazing!

Perhaps this desire to reveal more of himself than ever before helps account for the relative alacrity with which he agreed to these interviews. His press secretary, Madam Yeong Yoon Ying (or YY, as she is fondly addressed sometimes) says she cannot recall Minister Mentor giving a U.S. journalist this much interview time.

No, there must be something else underneath the surface of LKY, this ethnic Chinese man whose Singapore patriotism (and thus his political career) was born amid the horrific wartime Japanese occupation, and whose unbroken line of serial governments have led this strategically located island state of almost five million into an unexpectedly prominent destiny.

Who does *he* think he is?

He understands that he sometimes seems unapproachable, distant, even menacing.

I ask light-heartedly: "Will you greatly dispute me if I do not characterize you thusly, 'fun-loving' and 'light-hearted'?"

He shakes that off and answers un-defensively: "I would not call myself 'fun-loving' or 'light-hearted'. But I am not serious all the time. Everyone needs to have a good laugh now and then, to see the funny side of things, and to laugh at himself."

But I doubt many Singaporeans ever see his interior funny side. Maybe that's what he means when he says his people only know the exterior Lee.

This is not surprising. People often label Singapore the 'Nanny State'. It wakes you up in the morning, watches out for you during the day, and tucks you into bed at night. But it's necessarily a suffocating love, with little room for bubbly mirth.

But the 'Nanny State' appellation seems too un-masculine. Singapore puts a Darwinian emphasis on discipline and hard work. And looking over all is LKY, the ultimate godfather. To me, at least, the country has always seemed more like a 'Daddy State'. This reflection reminds me of an old American TV show—broadcasted decades ago—called "Father Knows Best".

It was a huge hit. The point of the storylines was that, yes, father did know best, even if the rest of the family sometimes did make fun of him behind his back. Many Americans watched admiringly, almost religiously. This was before America's feminists had made major inroads into U.S. culture. This was before the divorce rate soared, before gay marriage was a national political issue, and long before AIDS.

My own father, long deceased, had perhaps at least one quality in common with LKY: he was certain that this particular father did know best all the time. I am not entirely certain when I first knew of my ability to get along well with strong authoritarian figures who were always so sure of themselves. But it probably originated with the problem of getting along with my father. He was (shall we say?) not easy to get along with.

He was much taller than LKY, all German (as in Prussian, Poland-bound invasion type-A). He was poorly educated, but hard-working and decent, yet addicted to painkillers from wartime injury in the U.S. Marines, and as a teenager had been beaten sometimes on the back with an ice pick—by his father, who had (shall we say?) temper-control issues.

A lengthy conversation with my father was a rarity, and a negotiation. He also had a temper. He never hit me, though there was a time when I left the top off his after-shave lotion overnight that I thought I was done for.

My best friend in college was a bit like my father, too—mostly inaccessible, almost deliberately inept with small talk—but, like LKY, brilliant, in a quietly intimidating way. And then there were those overbearing father-knows-best bosses at *New York* magazine, *Time* magazine and a few other places where I worked but won't mention—demanding, unforgiving, difficult, though often (annoyingly) brilliant.

In truth, I was mostly comfortable with them.

I am always comfortable with LKY.

From him, you see, I don't expect fresh pastries, ballet music, a smell of saffron or an impromptu bout of standup comedy. To be fair, Minister Mentor Lee—at least in other interviews with him for my syndicated column prior to the far lengthier ones for this book—was always easier to talk to than my dad and always offered some of the very best interviews a journalist can have.

I find talking to him almost relaxing. Honest.

And, looking at this otherwise stalwart statesman, apparently having a bad health day, I now see he is dialing down into a slightly better mood. The heat compresses—one after another after another—seem to be soothing, and this interviewer from the West Coast of the U.S. hasn't irritated him with the usual nothing-is-new Western style questions about human rights, chewing gum and caning.

In fact, what Lee doesn't know (or maybe he does) is those questions seem less compelling to me precisely because they have been asked of him and his elite team over and over and over again.

The fact of the matter is that the country's prosperity and civility cannot be denied. What must be faced up to is this: Singapore is a huge success and an obvious gem (with imperfections, of course). We in the West may quarrel with the way it was achieved, but the achievement somehow seems to dwarf the critique. Why tear down a monument to hard work and smart decision-making? Singapore isn't about to invade neighboring states and impose its system on the unwilling. My goal in this book of conversations isn't to whittle

Singapore down to size, for whatever sadistic motive, but to size up the mentality and philosophy of modern Singapore's founder and see what can be learned.

Lee shifts his weight in his chair. He awaits.

Here we go: "I wanted to ask you about something that you've written about, which is your temperament, the anger issue that you attributed to your father who had such a temper." Rather than insult him by asking point-blank if he's a hothead, the question becomes the extent to which his alleged hot-headedness is inherited.

It is in this stormy context that Lee mentions his father in the first volume of his sweeping autobiography, *The Singapore Story*. I don't ask him to go too deep into this. Amateur psychoanalysis won't get us very far.

So we approach the temper issue from the perspective of policy pursuits rather than psychic permutations: "My theory is that your temper is primarily a tool of governance, leadership. Machiavelli —in your writings you do explicitly refer to Niccolò Machiavelli— said it was always best for the leader to be loved and feared, but if you can achieve but one, it is better to be feared than loved. So is temper a character defect or a tool of government?"

This seems the classy way of approaching it. After all, Hitler and Stalin had serious anger issues (then again, so did Gandhi and, well, Beethoven, not to mention Van Gogh and Von Karajan … and certainly Bill Clinton).

LKY seems to shift his weight a little. "If you can switch it on and off, yes, it can be a tool of government, but people with irrepressible tempers cannot switch it on and off. Now, because my father had a nasty temper, I decided that tempers are bad because it created unhappiness for my mother and for the family. So, I have never, I never try to lose my temper. Maybe I have occasionally, but I try to control it."

"You use it for effect, though, if you have to?" Frankly, this is one of the very few, if not only, times during the hours of interviewing that LKY, it seems to me, is being less than fully honest with himself.

"Seldom. If I am really angry, my body language will show that I am most dissatisfied."

"Can we say that you are almost like a young person growing up in an alcoholic family? They tend not to drink. You are saying it was a poisoned potion as far as you are concerned?"

It's not that I am thinking Lee is a liar. Being completely self-candid is hard for anyone. For years my regularly scheduled drinking of significant quantities of alcohol created problems, but it never occurred to me that what I was looking at was a truly serious drinking problem. But it occurred to my wife.

Lee pauses, then: "Yes, of course, and I have never struck my children which my father did. He took me by the ears and put me over the well because I'd rummaged his very precious Vaseline [brilliantine] called 4711, expensive in those days. I've never forgotten that. I read in the magazine, *American Scientific*, when something happens to you and it is traumatic, you'll never forget it."

Of course.

"I've never forgotten because I was only about four, five years old. So, I decided my father was a foolish man who never controlled himself."

And then me quickly inserting, noticing that all during this interview not a creature stirred outside in the corridor or around the interview table: "And then an uncontrolled temper is messy, right?"

"He made the whole family unhappy. He made my mother unhappy, and because of rows, all the children became unhappy. Confucianism requires me to support him [my father] in his old age, which I did."

The terms Confucianism and Asian values will crop up a lot in discussions with—and about—Lee. Roughly speaking, they mean a philosophy and ethics that lean toward traditional family-based and community-oriented values over modern technocratic and individual-centric ones. The achievement of Singapore has been to blend the two worlds together, though not without real pain. But his critics liken him to a Confucian emperor more than a democratically elected political figure. The knock on its founder is that he hides behind the old values (like his mother's skirt) whenever critics raise moral or ethical issues based on more individualistic, Western standards. What they may not understand is that no matter how Westernized Lee Kuan Yew became at Cambridge, his DNA is millennia-deep Chinese.

It seems unnecessary to push him further on the personal temper point. Everyone in the world knows he has one, whether controlled or otherwise. If he doesn't know this, then what's the point at this point? Every dry martini I take contains inherent unforeseen consequences. I still take one occasionally, but that's because even at my age, part of me is still a baby. All men are. Age is irrelevant. We guys tend to stay submerged in denial rather than surface and face certain deeply personal realities.

But, fool that I am, I push him one more time.

He nods, accepting that the book needs to be more personal if it is to add appreciably to what is known: "My faults are impatience in getting things done, pressing my associates and aides in putting in their best to get the job done, or fairly quickly replacing them when they are not making the effort well."

During the exchange, his two aides, seated at the other end of the table, say nothing and avert my eyes, despite my repeated staring. I am reasonably sure they are alive.

Lee adds: "I tend to blow up when my secretaries are dilatory and I am under pressure."

I wonder if there is anything else.

"This is not an exhaustive list. I cannot see myself."

There is a silence.

He adds: "My faults are many and numerous. You will have to ask my opponents and enemies, and there are many in Singapore."

The Fox and the Hedgehog
(Not a Disney Movie)

WHAT IS THE temper of the times? What is the temper/distemper of the leader? When one thinks of an authoritarian leader (however 'soft') who sports a bad temper, one thinks of a Hitler or a Hirohito leading a militarily powerful country.

But what about one leading a militarily insignificant country?

The Pope was not to be feared, Stalin once said. After all, how many divisions has he got?

But world influence cannot be measured in the mere metrics of military capabilities. Pope John Paul II (Karol Wojtyla) helped end the Cold War through the barrel of steady moral barrages against Communism. Lee, also a staunch anti-communist, has had regional and international influence through the potency of his ideas about governance, culture and international relations—ideas that have special force in part because his country Singapore has put many of them into action. Ask almost anyone, even some of his enemies, and they will almost all agree: Lee is a giant of Asia, no matter how tiny his country.

I draw his attention to a famous essay, decades old, by the late great Oxford Fellow Isaiah Berlin that may provide a key to unlock the secret of the mind of LKY. It's about how one might classify great figures in history. An analogy from Greek literature of the hedgehog and the fox is used to divide great men and women into two major categories of great leaders.

As he hunches up a little in his chair, I explain it goes like this: *the Fox knows lots of things, lots of different ways of surviving. The Hedgehog only knows one major thing, but the one that the Hedgehog knows is a really big deal—it is central to his life and that of everyone else.*

So Einstein, who brought forth into the world this huge idea (about universal relativity), would obviously be a Hedgehog. By contrast, the genius Aristotle was the scientist of thousands of little ideas and thus arguably would be the Fox who knew lots of little things. Both are geniuses, but of different kinds.

"Now, in this famous book, Berlin moves quickly into talking about what he really wants to talk about, which is the great novelist Leo Tolstoy. What is the nature of Tolstoy's genius? Berlin asks himself. Did Tolstoy think he was a Fox or did Tolstoy think he was a Hedgehog? And, even then, was Tolstoy not just underestimating himself? It seems to me you are almost adamant in saying that you are a Fox, that you know a lot of little practical things, and you are not bringing to the world some big Hedgehog idea."

In other words, this is our main question: LKY—Hedgehog, or Fox? And it is the big thematic question to which we will return at the end of our conversations.

Listening carefully, he lets out a faint sigh and tightens the heat pad on his right thigh, then says: "I don't think in those terms.

I am not great on philosophy and theories. I am interested in them, but my life is not guided by philosophy or theories. I get things done and leave others to extract the principles from my successful solutions. I do not work on a theory. Instead I ask: what will make this work? If, after a series of such solutions, I find that a certain approach worked, then I try to find out what was the principle behind the solution."

My sense is that Lee harbors the gut instinct that all general political theories, however expressed by (say) the average otherwise harmless university professor, contain either an explosive measure of danger or an ocean of profound naiveté. For when pushed to logical end points, they incline toward extremism, whether Communism at its purest or a brutal brand of capitalism sometimes labeled 'free-market fundamentalism' or ... (most probably of all) toward inconsequentialism.

Lee works through these thoughts: "So, Plato, Aristotle, Socrates, I am not guided by them. I read them cursorily because I was not interested in philosophy as such. You may call me a 'utilitarian' or whatever. I am interested in what works."

> I am not great on philosophy and theories. I am interested in them, but my life is not guided by philosophy or theories.

Lee then uses a deft example to demonstrate the advantages of keeping your ideology from running away with your common sense. "So, back in the 1960s, 1970s, 1980s," he says, a touch dismissively, "when the conventional and fashionable theories held [so-called] 'Third World leaders' in thrall, 'socialism', 'Communism', 'the Soviet Republic' and 'no exploiting multinationals', I bucked the trend and succeeded. Then the others in the region followed my example."

Third World ideology took the unwavering (indeed, the mind-blowingly ideological) view that permitting a foreign multinational corporation to operate in your country was to hand them the key to the Treasury, allow them to bilk the country's natural resources and steal off with your most talented children. In Singapore, though, the country possessed splendid human resources, not to mention a vigilant and cagey LKY watching over the massive multinationals, to keep their predatory practices to a minimum.

He is clear enough on his pragmatism, but, whether he accepts it or not, extreme pragmatic utilitarianism is itself a philosophy: "And so you brought to your political culture a new utilitarian religion!"

Barely missing a beat, for the moment ignoring my off-center direction, he went on: "What is my guiding principle? Presented with the difficulty or major problem or an assortment of conflicting facts, I review what alternatives I have if my proposed solution doesn't work. I choose a solution which offers a higher probability of success, but if it fails, I have some other way. Never a dead end."

"I see. There's always a Plan B so you can always get off Plan A real fast?"

"Yes, of course, if it doesn't work."

"And you will not let lobbyists and other vested interests keep it at Point A if it is not good for the country?"

"Right. No!"

So, working with the multinationals, he is an anti-Marxist, right? That's sort of an ideology, a Hedgehog idea, right? I ask him.

His response: "I am not anti-Marxist but anti-communist, i.e. anti-Leninist methods of organizing a party to capture power and to hold a society in its total grip once in power."

Critics sometimes suggest that Lee's People's Action Party (PAP) is semi-Leninist in character. But the central government's method of control is far more subtle and not remotely as brutal; and it derives credibility from the dramatically positive economic and societal results produced. Western commentators who can discern little difference between LKY and Fidel Castro have much to learn about Singapore's founder.

He goes on: "Marx argues that labor creates excess returns that are creamed off by capitalists. But Marx was wrong when he predicted this would lead to great injustices and, finally, rebellion and a collapse of the capitalist system. This has not happened because of trade unions fighting for better working conditions, and governments redistributing incomes through housing, health, education and social security benefits."

All this is to the good, he suggests, especially the use of central government intervention to sand down the rough edges of capitalism. It keeps things moving forward. But extended to an ideology, or to some inflexible formula (or political party platform), state interventionism can be dangerous.

In this regard, he worries a lot about the direction of the U.S. He adds: "In Europe, because the social security net is over-generous, the workers are not as hard driving and the economy has become sluggish. The U.S. is at the other end, higher competition, with less social support. However, if the Obama administration and Congress move towards the European model of social support, it will lead to a slower and less dynamic American economy."

As we do and shall see even more clearly, Lee is hardly shy about putting up Stop Signs and offering advice to others. He obviously enjoys being the Sage of Singapore, though he's smart enough not to charge foolishly into dangerous waters. In past interviews he would sometimes decline a leading question by saying something like, "No, no, no, I don't want to get into a fight on that point with your American Congress."

> You may call me a 'utilitarian' or whatever. I am interested in what works.

What's certainly true of the Singapore sage is the high quality of his counsel. It is balanced. He is no religious believer in free-market fundamentalism. He would never fall for the primitivism that humans are always rational and/or self-interested actors whose behavior can be modeled with predictive precision and whose decisions are always in their and/or their society's best interests.

I ask: "So where do your core instincts originate from?"

"You can begin by analyzing my character. My thinking comes from my character. How did I get to be what I am? Maybe my DNA was that way. Also I have my life experiences. One meets a series of unforeseeable and unpredictable situations when your whole world collapses. Anyway, mine did. The British Empire was supposed to last another 1,000 years in Southeast Asia, but collapsed when the Japanese army came in 1942. I never thought they could conquer Singapore and push the British out. They did, and brutalized us, including me. Luckily, my head was not cut off. Many lost theirs."

"You had a narrow escape at one point."

He nods affirmatively.

"I learned about power long before Mao Zedong wrote that power came from the barrel of the gun. The Japanese demonstrated this; the British did not. They [the Brits] were at the tail end of Empire when they did not have to use brute force. The British had superiority in technology, commerce and knowledge. They built this big Government House on a hill with Indian convict labor in 1868 to dominate the populations. This building dominated the whole island. I learned how to govern, how you dominate the people, as the British did, and how the Japanese used their power.

"The moment the Japanese took over, they moved to all the big buildings. They became the dominant force, and with the power of life and death over you, you obey, or no food, arrest, torture. The whole population became submissive except for a few who took to the jungle and fought back as guerillas and, if they were caught…"

"Tortured, huh?"

He coughs again.

"Yeah, many were. You can say, I am a 'Fox' in the sense that I know in this situation, this happens, in that situation, that happens. Watch your step, like the fox."

"And you know a lot of survival steps, right?"

He nods: "But is there a guiding principle, a golden thread that runs through all of them? I am not sure, I am not sure."

I push on, determined or foolish, I don't really know: "Just to underline that point, but that's exactly what Isaiah Berlin gets at with regard to Leo Tolstoy, and Tolstoy sounds just like you. Seriously! Tolstoy in effect said, I don't have a general principle, I don't have an over-arching philosophical approach, I want the empirical data, I want the specifics and then I respond as necessary … like that. But Berlin's thesis is that precisely because Tolstoy was a genius, the geniuses always, even subconsciously, look for some unifying principle or, perhaps, some sense of overall order. You know what I mean, so that you don't really have to make your overall framework up all the time."

Just as Berlin thought Tolstoy was a secret Hedgehog, no matter what the great Russian novelist thought of himself, I harbor the same instinct about Singapore's modern founder. But I know he portrays himself as a sensible-shoes British empiricist without theoretical pretensions, and so I know my Tolstoy Hedgehog idea is destined to prove a hard sell to this hard-boiled statesman. But why give up so soon? We Americans are born optimists!

How about Plato? I ask him whether his beloved Singapore (the country, not the movie) properly wants to be a later-day

Republic in the fashion of Plato—elitist, meritocratic, learned, anti-one-man-one-vote. He knows you wouldn't be able to get Plato to endorse the idea that the homeless man in the gutter of the street should have the same one vote as the president of Harvard.

I say: "And if you did have a system that could produce a Plato, whose idea of the city-state was as close to utopia as one might get on earth, wouldn't you want Plato to run your country?"

Lee clears his throat, as if at the same time clearing his mind, but pushes the focus away from Singapore and toward the larger question of superior governance and stable world order: "Plato talked in terms of a city-state. We are talking in terms of mega-nations with many ethnic groups, many cultures, many religions, multiple contradictions between them. How it will pan out, I cannot say, but I do know that the present system is not, as [the American political economist Francis] Fukuyama believes, the end of history, that nothing else can excel democracy, that you cannot displace it. That's not true."

I say: "Classic liberal democracies may even take us to a dead end. I mean, I have spent four, five months now reading all your stuff and thinking about what you've said and preparing for this interview, and I see you as doing a number of things. But on the Hedgehog side, your whole implicit critique of democracy, of one-man, one-vote, I think your views, which in America would be deemed politically incorrect, to say the least, arise from a deep well of good will, as well as genuine fear. I don't think they are evil in any sense. You stand for good governance. I mean if you stand for anything at all, you stand for good governance."

Next you will hear—loud and clear—the voice of the no-nonsense British utilitarian.

"Every society wants to be governed by leaders who bring the greatest good to the greatest number in a fair and non-discriminating way. We could not have held the society together if we had not made adjustments to the system that gives the Malays, although they are not as hardworking and capable as the other races, a fair share of the cake. Their lives are improving, they have got their own homes, more are receiving tertiary education and becoming professionals in various fields. They're improving because they see their neighbors pushing their children in education and so that helps."

This is where LKY is only hinting at a long and deeply held conviction that might be termed 'negative eugenics'. Just as careful breeding in the animal world can produce superior specimens, careless inbreeding in the animal (and human) world can produce less capable or less gifted subcultures. He views the rural Malays with compassion, but also with conviction: they are not bred to be go-getters. He has comparable views about the Uighurs, who have been pushed around by a massive influx of ethnic Han Chinese into Xinjiang, in western China. To reduce the sometimes violent tensions there, as on the Malay Peninsula, the answer is economic development that benefits all, even when you have to tweak the wealth-distribution machine in new ways.

He says: "They [the Chinese government] develop Xinjiang

and they believe they will alleviate the problem. I told one of their ministers that when I went to Urumqi, the capital in Xinjiang in 1990, I found the Uighurs in the majority, over 50 percent, and all in low-rise buildings. When this trouble broke out, Uighurs were now only 14 percent of the population of Urumqi and the Han Chinese are over 70 percent in these tall buildings. The roads and development have brought in the Han Chinese from the coastal cities. How can these Uighurs compete with the Hans?

"I told them, look, why don't you do it another way? You can't make the Uighur competitive in business as the Chinese have been doing this for thousands of years. Why not get your Han companies to bring the best of the Uighurs in as minority partners? Then they are also in the high-rises and also sharing in the growth. Instead, they are being pushed out, not just their big companies, but even their hawkers and small shopkeepers, squeezed out. If I were a Uighur, I would feel the Hans are taking over. Infrastructure development means more Han Chinese. More Han Chinese … doesn't matter if I get richer as a result, but I'm becoming poorer."

Ethnicities and nationalities that are allowed to be set at one another's throats strike Lee as governance gone stupid. The more integrated they are than ghettoized, economically as well as politically, the better for economic development, not to mention political stability. He grabs another contemporary example out of the air, as if reaching for a few bars of some musical score to illustrate a favorite, if commonsensical, theme.

"Another example is Sri Lanka. It is not a happy, united country. Yes, they [the majority Sinhalese government] have beaten the Tamil Tigers this time, but the Sinhalese who are less capable are putting down a minority of Jaffna Tamils who are more capable. They were squeezing them out. That's why the Tamils rebelled. But I do not see them ethnic cleansing all two million-plus Jaffna Tamils. The Jaffna Tamils have been in Sri Lanka as long as the Sinhalese."

"So what Asia saw was ethnic cleansing?"

"That's right."

"They will come back, you think?"

"I don't think they are going to be submissive or go away. The present president of Sri Lanka believes he has settled the problem; his Tamil Tigers are killed and that is that."

I look up from my notes and with a sense that here we might be seeing a side of LKY that is under-reported, I say: "See, that's really a fascinating point, because to the extent that we have any sense of who you are at all, we think of you as this hard-boiled force-first guy. But in fact your system of government is much softer, consensual and intelligent, whereas what the Sinhalese in Sri Lanka are doing is a caricature of an LKY who never existed."

Lee fights a cringe, as if fighting off a bad memory—or my bad analogy. He starts to say something, then stops, then leaves it at this, referring to Sri Lanka's president: "I've read his speeches and I knew he was a Sinhalese extremist. I cannot change his mind."

Undertaking battles that cannot be won is not a particular

trademark of LKY's pragmatic success formula. Neither is a religious obeisance to so-called pure democracy as the form of preferred government. He does not mention that Sri Lanka is a democracy, based on one-citizen, one-vote. He's not against democracies when they work. He's against defending them just because they are democracies. This position strikes me as more consistent than the U.S. relationship with other democracies: we support them only when we approve of them, denouncing them (or worse) when we don't.

He is also opposed to defending propositions that have little factual foundation simply because they are politically correct. He does think, by and large, Chinese people work harder than many other nationalities or ethnicities (though not, for example, more than the Japanese). In fact, he suspects the 21st century will be a Chinese or Asian one. He thinks the Tamils deserve more respect than the Sinhalese have given them. He doubts the average Malay will ever become a hard-charging workaholic, as are many Chinese … as are (as we will see later) many Israelis … and as are the Japanese. In fact, the Japanese are so driven that they serve to underscore the point that even an inefficient democratic system of government is not necessarily an impediment to economic growth.

China Syndrome

THE SINGAPORE-CHINA relationship is an important part of this conversation. But first a little background is needed.

LKY would be the first to admit that he is riveted by China. After his Singapore, he probably thinks about nothing else more, though rising India has lately been high on his radar screen.

China is not just a huge place almost beyond human imagination, but it also has become a huge new concept. For the first time in a long time, all our futures will depend a lot on what China does or does not do. This will be tough for many of us in the West, especially, to digest. We are used to being center-stage.

China is not only a country with more inhabitants than any other. Now rising to re-establish its normal high ranking in the planet's geopolitical universe, it is also an icon for breakneck economic development. Unstoppable? No one knows; anything can happen, and in China, it has. But it does look to be the Asian express train of the 21st century. This was not the vision of the future back in the 1960s, when it was still a stumbling, half-sleeping giant. But deeply embedded historical forces do not stay down for long.

It has been the instinct of LKY and his inner circle to try to look beyond (and be publicly articulate about looking beyond) history's next great breathtaking, hairpin curve. Much like the great thinker Arnold J. Toynbee (1889–1975), his sense is that civilizations and cultures need (more or less urgently) to respond to the challenges and threats of history, if they are to survive. He also shares the view with Toynbee that a culture or country that lacks a driving, highly educated elite deeply committed to public service is doomed to be slow to respond—perhaps tragically and even fatally slow.

On one level, Lee's huge bets on the elitist approach to governance can be attributed to his DNA debt, as it were, to the track record of highly effective Chinese Mandarins in past dynasties. But beyond mere reprise, Lee's contemporary power elite represents an affirmation and extension of that principle in a very different set of circumstances. In effect, modern governance, which includes basic decision-making and priority-setting, is too complex to be left to the man in the street.

Lee always knew that his obsession about China was in Singapore's long-term national interest. If a tiny vulnerable country like Singapore doesn't climb aboard and perhaps even slip into a seat behind the pilot-engineer on the Chinese train, operating as a kind of unofficial back-seat driver, it will be left dangerously behind. He has also steadily obsessed that if China itself didn't change dramatically, that train would never even leave the station—and the whole region would be stuck without this huge economic engine.

Quick as … well … a fox, LKY climbed aboard, ran into the cabin, and began engaging with Deng Xiaoping (1904–97). The

late master leader of China—the successor to Mao Zedong—
saved China from total collapse. The former prime minister of
Singapore may 'only' be a Fox, by his own estimation, but Deng
was a Hedgehog if there ever was one. Deng came to accept the
very large idea that only some kind of reformed entrepreneurial
capitalism could save communist China from self-destruction.
He had that 'vision thing', as we say in the U.S.

The two leaders had in common extreme ambition, a
determination not to let anything or anyone get in their way, and
a shared sense of the Chinese people, everywhere, deserving a special
place on the world stage. They first met when the diminutive, chain-
smoking Deng, 74 years old, was still nowhere yet near the height
of his powers on the mainland. Lee, from the colossally smaller
country south of the Malay Peninsula, was then approximately two
decades younger and well into his powers over Singapore, though
not so well known on the global stage. This was in 1978. The timing
is important to appreciate. Lee was worried about Singapore being
left behind when China got back up to speed.

The near-epochal Deng-Lee get-together did not finally occur
until a half-dozen years after the stunning February 1972 secret
visit of Richard Nixon to China. As screamingly cynical a move
for both sides of the Sino-U.S. aisle as the Nixon ploy was, it
yielded the pivotal Shanghai Communiqué. This pledged the
governments of the United States and the People's Republic of
China to work toward the normalization of relations and not "seek
hegemony in the Asia-Pacific region". Few American diplomatic

about-faces had ever so stunned the world. And for Asia, it was nothing less than a major political earthquake. Today, Lee, in particular—though hardly uniquely, of course—views 1972 as a positive watershed year in the evolution of the strategic structure of East-West relations.

In Lee's eyes, President Richard Nixon carved out a special place for himself in history. That is, he may have been inept in a hundred smaller ways, but not on this very big issue of China. The sins of Watergate and other serious errors of judgment notwithstanding, Nixon, for one, at least understood the big ideas that make the world go around. For a long time prior to that breakthrough, the best policy wisdom about China was that the sleeping giant should be fed tranquilizers with its daily slathering of shark-fin soup to keep it sleepy. But Nixon sensed that China would not sleep forever, and those who did not try to use China for its own national interests would inevitably lose the game to those that did. Trying to ally Beijing against Moscow, which was then the enormously menacing Soviet Empire, seemed like a very good idea at the time.

Lee greatly admired the hard geopolitical groundwork of Nixon and his then-national security advisor Henry Kissinger. And as Mao began to come to his end, Lee reached out to Deng in as seemly a way as possible. By 1978 Deng was itching to get the country moving forward—and fast. His visit to Singapore then became known as something of a widely heralded crash-course in rapid state-driven, capitalistic economic development, with Lee as Friendly Collegial Tutor. When Deng ended the visit and went on to other stops, he complimented Lee on Singapore's impressive achievements. Lee said thank you for the compliment, but of course both understood that Singapore was scarcely a third or a fourth the population of Shanghai alone. Lee says that Deng sighed and replied with something like: "If I only had Shanghai to do, I too might be able to change Shanghai quickly [as you have Singapore]. But I have the whole of China!"

Tiny or little titan, you have to admire the way small Singapore, being demographically two-thirds Chinese, became the smarty-pants tutor in the re-education of Deng, the master rebuilder of massive China. This tutorial role has been an immensely positive factor in Singapore's prestigious rise in Asia—and one of a number of important factors in China's lusty embrace of a kind of socialized capitalism. The true measure of Lee's influence on China's tilt toward a kind of Chinese capitalism can of course be overstated, but it can also be understated. For few dispute that China was desperate for models that were (a) Chinese and (b) success stories. There weren't too many of them in 1978. One was Singapore—and the place was in Asia, not in Scandinavia; it was Chinese, not Japanese or Occidental; and it was a winner.

Lee nods: "The Chinese know I have helped them in the past. The ideas that Deng Xiaoping formed, if he had not come here [in the 1970s] and seen the Western multinationals in Singapore producing wealth for us, training our people so as a result we were able to build a prosperous society, then he might never have opened up ... opening up the coastal SEZs [Special Economic Zones] that eventually led to the whole of China opening up by joining the World Trade Organization.

"He had fortuitously seen Singapore. In 1978, we had a discourse. I said to him, Communism will only work if you believe that all men will sacrifice themselves for their fellow men and not [first] for themselves and their families. I work on the basis that all men and women first work for themselves and their families, and only then will they share a portion of it with the less fortunate. That's the basis on which I work."

Lee, in effect, is claiming a role (which magnitude to be determined by history's later judgment) in helping lay the groundwork for what may turn out to be a Chinese century.

"So, he decided, lease the land to the farmers, individual farmers, whereupon productivity went up. He must have been thinking about it, but seeing Singapore confirmed his thinking. It worked well in the coastal provinces, SEZs, especially Shenzhen, tapping Hong Kong. Then all the cities opened up. Now, the whole country is in WTO."

And I add the very obvious point: "Which was a huge historical jump and political decision."

Right, he nods: "So, the relationship with me goes back a long way, opening windows for them. When they deal with my successors, it's different. The Chinese are already successful. But since they can still learn from our system, they still visit us."

This is a key point with LKY, and central to understanding the proposition that Singapore's importance must transcend its size and population. Instead of cowering and feeling diminished in the shadow of giants, this microwave-size nation gains stature by playing with the big boys, even somewhat fearlessly, though never recklessly.

He looks at me with that pair of raisin-black eyes and quickly adds: "It is silly to think they will just copy us. They look at us and say, well, will this work in China? Where they think something will work, they take that particular segment and bud-graft it onto their system with some alterations."

He goes into detail about a specific Singapore policy that works in China: "Take their housing program for public housing. [Then Chinese Vice Premier] Zhu Rongji came here in 1990, and he went into the bolts and nuts with us: how did you succeed in getting a whole population to own their own apartments? He studied our system; we had a Central Provident Fund with individual accounts and you pay 20 percent of your salary, your employer pays 20 percent. Out of that account, you can pay your installments for your home over a 30-year period. A portion of the CPF is kept for their 'Medisave'; medical care requires co-payments so people don't go to hospitals or clinics for frivolous reasons. Zhu Rongji started something similar for housing in Shanghai."

"Did the Singapore health insurance approach work in Shanghai?"

"Yeah, it's working and copied with variation, and with further modification for different parts of China."

I ask him to compare the late Deng with the very recent Zhu

Rongji, who until 2003 was the Number Two in China and the much-acclaimed technical virtuosi of China's most recent economic reforms and plunge into the WTO: "In modern times in China, isn't Zhu Rongji the sort of spiritual successor to Deng Xiaoping as a pragmatist?"

LKY thinks that one over a bit, re-adjusts the pad, looks out toward his right where the long corridor leads to his office, then says: "The veterans of the Long March do not really understand the free market. They may have read Adam Smith in translation, but what they knew best was the communist system. It brought China down. Deng could see the Soviet Union, Cuba and Eastern Europe. He was looking for a way out of this. Singapore was a useful source for a different working system for them, best with adjustments."

> I work on the basis that all men and women first work for themselves and their families, and only then will they share a portion of it with the less fortunate.

Without at all diminishing the brilliant Zhu, Lee cannot escape the pull of Deng as the communist who in effect broke with Communism—a gigantic leap of leadership.

I counter, trying to bring the matter into the useful present: "How about this, then? We think of it as Singapore seedlings, little parts of your national experience can be transplanted and can sprout in compatible soils elsewhere. How does that metaphor work for you?"

Lee doesn't disapprove and refers to the famous Suzhou project on the Chinese mainland: "I don't know if you have been to Suzhou. It's their best township, well laid out, beautiful, by a lake. We chose the site. It was farming land, a 70-square kilometre [27-square mile] site, and we had much trouble because they were poor at that time so they made us carry all the overheads, the infrastructure. We paid for moving the power lines out of the land, and for connecting the site to the main highway."

He sighs, adjusting the heat pad with some irritation: "We had to bear the cost; we lost money. We brought over 2,000 of their officials to Singapore to learn and when they went back, our officials went with them. Suzhou is now their prized project. Other provinces are going there, learning from them and they are very proud of it. They have just celebrated the 15th anniversary. They invited me, brought out all the old ministers and the present minister in charge to attend and publicize it, which is for them good and for us, too, good because after it was completed, at first they advertised in the *Financial Times* that this project came about without Singapore, just Suzhou. They did it all by themselves. But until we got involved, the investors didn't come."

I say: "Is that right?"

"Then they put it out as a Singapore-Suzhou *joint* venture. Then the investors came. The Chinese asked us, 'Please, don't leave.' "

"Because the Singapore addition is the guarantee of standards?" In America we would call it the Good Housekeeping Seal of Approval!

He nods: "We gave it credibility. What is interesting is because if you say to most Americans, even those who have been to Harvard, if you say to them, Singapore is excellent, they will say, well, how big is Singapore? Well, I say, four million people, okay. But then one can say, but Singapore has had an influence on, not a control of, but an influence on, China for reasons XYZ, and those reasons XYZ are generally good for everybody, the world, and then, now, they are more interested."

That's a rather convincing way of describing it.

For many Americans, however, helping China get on its feet after centuries of relative sleep and seeing it wake up with a roar is disconcerting.

We joke about whether he might be a closet communist after all!

He laughs and says: "William Safire [the legendary former *New York Times* op-ed columnist who died in September 2009] thought I was a dangerous fellow, teaching the Chinese how to do things! Why do you want the communists to succeed? Well, even some of my own officers told me, look, why do we teach them and then they will outdo us and then we are in trouble?

"So, I told them, this is a chance for us to get a foot in China at a time when they don't know how to do it. But they've got so many bright fellows and they are going to go all around the world, and you can't prevent them from coming to Singapore with a camcorder and taking pictures and studying us. So, we might as well do this for them; make a great impact on them and the leadership.

"Now we have one foot in China. And so we have got a joint committee that meets once a year, their vice premier and our deputy prime minister. We have started an eco-city in Tianjin, which will take 15 more years to do. We are engaged at various levels; they are sending 110 to 120 mayors, or officials on the mayor level, every year from all their cities, to a course here for eight to nine months on public administration and urban management. We run the course in Chinese for them, and then they go round and study and we see them right back in their own cities writing about their experience here, which is not bad. It gives us a good reputation in Chinese cities."

The Perfect Storm

SURVIVAL WORRIES: if Singapore is not attached to forces bigger than Singapore, it will become smaller, could shrink and might even be absorbed by a larger country—and thus die. Lee talks often about the need for his little Singapore to see—and act on—the bigger picture.

"Shell Oil, the multinational, once gave me the idea for the term 'helicopter quality'. In other words, you can see a problem in total and you can zero in on the detail, which you have to see to solve, and zoom on it. That's called helicopter quality. Now, if you are too low, your helicopter quality is too low, you do not see the whole picture nor can your zoom be powerful."

Hmmm: "Okay, but as you come up from the helicopter and you are seeing the bigger picture, what does that mean, the bigger picture?" I am still groping for a Hedgehog hint from him.

He senses the intellectual undertow—that I am trying to whoosh him out into deeper waters—but he is quick and nimble and digs his feet further in the sand: "The bigger picture means you can see this part as part of something else. I mean, you take Singapore. Singapore does not exist in isolation. What you see in Singapore is a reflection of the world it lives in, it is the world it is connected with. So, the world it is connected with widens with technology. Sailing ships, East India Company needed a watering place for their ships to go to China, from India to China. Finally, they've got opium to give to the Chinese and bits of silver. Then came the steamship, faster, more connections. Then came the Suez Canal, better still. Then came faster ships, then came the flying boats. Then came cables. Now, optic fiber, broadband. As the world changes, we are more and more connected."

He sometimes talks the way his mind reasons—jabbing forward for intellectual position like a prizefighter trying to push uncertainty into a corner for the kill.

"So, the bigger picture now is this. Our fate does not depend just on what goes on in Johor or in Indonesia or in ASEAN [Association of Southeast Asian Nations]. It depends on what happens in America in this new order now. Thirty years ago, I would say Americas, Europe, Japan, they were the developed dynamos in the world. Gradually, that changed. Today, there is still America Number One, Japan Number Two, Europe Number Three, and the potential now is China, Number Four, likely to be Number Two in about 20 years, and India today, Number Seven or so, likely to be one behind China in 20, 30 years. So, you must factor that into your calculations as you are going forward in your policy.

> Our fate does not depend just on what goes on in Johor or in Indonesia or in ASEAN. It depends on what happens in America in this new order now.

Because in the 1970s, I could see that China, once it changes its system, was bound to rise. Because when I went there and I talked to them, I found very capable minds, of course then blinkered by their ideology."

Dumb feet-in-cement Hedgehogs, Lee was probably thinking to himself, they'd be better off being a more flexible Fox like me.

Me saying: "Sure, held back by the system."

LKY nods vigorously: "Yes, by the system, the communist system. So, I said, well, we'd better, whilst they need us, we had better help them, then we've got a foot in, which has happened. But riding with China alone will put us in hot weather."

Like the little jungle bird that looks for safety by riding on the back of a giant hippopotamus while pecking away helpfully at the big monster's annoying little insect issues, Singapore has more than one hippo it aims to ride. There's emerging India, for another. Then—Lee says not to forget—there's still Japan, with its still-giant economy.

But let's linger on China.

For a long time, America only knew China by the extraordinary work of Pearl Buck, whose novel *The Good Earth* was practically viewed as a tourist guidebook on the Chinese peasant soul. She became the first American woman to win the Nobel Prize for Literature.

So I put it to him this way: "*The Good Earth* stirred a really deep feeling among Americans that the Chinese people possess some kind of eternal soul no matter the political system under which they suffer. You have touched on this. You have said Mao Zedong may have had 100 sayings and all kinds of newfangled ideas, but there are 5,000 years of more or less continuous civilization before him, and so there are five million other sayings. So one wonders, the 600 million people in the Chinese countryside, those who are not along the coasts and the cities, are they still Pearl Buck's peasants despite all the voracious economic development?"

Lee seems to like this question, mulls it over like a wine connoisseur lovingly opening an unfamiliar new bottle. He then grabs the heat pad like Linus huddling a blanket, the hacking cough reminding us that time stops for no man.

"Yes, but with this difference now, and I put it at two levels. One is what sociologists call low culture, your basic beliefs and your attitudes to things. I mean, after the first month of childbirth, you don't do these things and you must eat these things and so on. That low culture persists, the way they are being governed in those areas of China, but where the officials are squeezing them for extra taxes and so on, they now have cell phones and they find out that this is not the central government doing this but the local officials. They've got the knowledge, so they're no longer as submissive.

"So, you find clashes with the police and so on because the police are made use of by the lower officials, who push the rural people from their land at cheap prices and then they sell it at a profit to the commercial people who want to build big factories or houses.

"So, there is now a growing farming population with more knowledge of the way the country is because they've also got children running away and working in the coastal cities and many have gone back now, millions and millions of them … and so they have brought back the knowledge of the outside world, of their city life."

Knowingly or not, it seems to me, Lee is painting a classic portrait of a pre-revolutionary situation: "So, China is gradually changing profoundly. Increasingly cheap and available technology and cascades of reverse migration are wising people up to the true story of the exploitation of China's heretofore isolated rural regions.

"And, furthermore, the Chinese know that with their industrialization, every year, ten or plus millions will go into the new towns they are constructing for their people. So, they have prepared ten new towns of 40 million persons each."

That is one breathtaking scenario, I say: "The most unbelievable aspect of China is just the sheer numbers … of everything. Is the Middle Kingdom going to be able to hold the whole all together?"

Lee saying: "If they change in a pragmatic way, as they have been doing, keeping tight security control and not allowing riots and not allowing rebellions and at the same time, easing up, you know, giving more provincial authority, more city authority, more grassroots power, it's holdable."

Please note that LKY equates tight security with national

security. Conversely, easing up politically might trigger an unraveling. The Western perspective views official crackdowns critically; Lee sees them as unavoidable for a country of that size, history and degree of unsolved problems.

How can they pull that off—I wonder—without significant psychological, mental and ideological changes within the overarching Communist Party?

Lee nods: "Yes, of course. Their first hindrance, which is something they have not contemplated doing, is to remove the privileges of the 70 million members of the Communist Party. You can commit any crime; you cannot be investigated by the Public Procurator. Only the Party Disciplinary Committee can punish you. So, the Disciplinary Committee is influenced by, you know, which faction is this chap supporting? I mean, you don't want to punish a chap who is supporting you. So, that is one of the reasons why the corruption has not been weeded out."

I wonder out loud whether it is at least imaginable that the Chinese Communist Party will evolve out of its original control-all ambition into something like Japan's Liberal Democratic Party. This was the huge umbrella structure that until last year [2009] ruled the Japanese polity like an octopus with tentacles hungrily grabbing at every unoccupied space.

LKY doubts the analogy.

"No, because the tradition is different, the history is different. The Japanese system grew out of the samurais, the samurai with X number of followers who will die for me or die with me. So, when they get together, samurais get together and each brings his followers."

Me saying: "Those are the famous factions of the LDP."

"Yeah. So, they brought that into their political system, their faction system, and [the] head of the faction finds the resources to shower on the other MPs. Otherwise, you cannot be a faction leader. You must have the money to support them. Every time an election takes place, it costs five million dollars. Their salaries and all the perks come up to nearly 100 million dollars. So, when election comes, you've got to find the money."

Lee means a whole lot of money—yards and yards of yen.

"The [historic] Chinese system is different. In the imperial system, the leader, or the emperor, appoints all the senior officials. How are they appointed? Through the examination system. Whether the examination produces good administrators or not, it's questionable, but it produces very brainy people. So, the Communist Party has modernized that system. After the Cultural Revolution, they went back to that model. They put it down that (and Deng Xiaoping started this) at such and such an age, you retire from this job; at that age, you retire, and even if you get to the Central Committee and the Politburo, you retire 65, or if you are the chief, the president or the prime minister, you retire at 70.

"So, each new crop now is more highly educated than the last one. You get mayors now who've got PhDs and some of them, MBAs from American universities. Therefore, there is no faction as such but just loyalties to different leaders within the leadership."

"And you don't think that the Chinese will allow their Central Party to evolve into a faction-driven dynamic?"

"They know this, that if you break China up this way, it will fall apart."

The counter-argument is that China in fact will fall apart if the Communist Party doesn't drop dogmatic homogeneity, and develop open and vigorously competing schools of thought that better reflect honest differences of opinion across the great expanse of China. It seems so obvious, to me anyway.

The Good,
the Bad and the Ugly

LKY'S VIEW OF the dynamics behind contemporary historical events is complex. As any sophisticated man or woman knows, no one factor can explain all that happens in life, whether economics, game theory, culture, or even a Higher Power. But he is certain that great leaders at the top of their game can push history in desirable directions. Because he is a proponent of government elitism—always assuming the elite is highly qualified, deeply motivated and un-craven, which is one assumption—it is logical that he would find value in the Great Man Theory of History.

"Who were some other great men you've met?"

"I would say the greatest was Deng Xiaoping. At his age, to admit that he was wrong, that all these ideas, Marxism, Leninism, Maoism, they are just not working and have to be abandoned, you need a great man to do that and to convince or override his Old Guard colleagues and say, now we go this different way."

Many Westerners would gasp at the thought of putting Deng on such a pedestal. After all, the most powerful communist leader since Mao was a known killer of political opponents. When he served under Mao he oversaw executions, gulags and famines made far more deadly by murderous state indifference. As Mao's successor, he was the power at the throne in 1989, infamously pulling the trigger at Tiananmen Square that left at least several thousand unarmed Chinese civilians dead.

These well-known facts notwithstanding, Lee's admiration is driven by an appreciation of Deng's boldness in abandoning the debilitating ideology of communist economics for a mélange of opportunistic neo-capitalist or classic-entrepreneurial reforms. The historic effort was to wind up lifting hundreds of millions of Chinese out of poverty and bringing realistic hope to China for the first time in a very long time. The Singapore leader's apparent tolerance of all things Deng may at times seem shocking, but it is consistent with his larger view that methods of government vary from culture to culture, and cannot be condemned out of hand if the net result is steady and/or dramatic improvement in the lot of the people. As a kind of pessimistic progressive, he doubts that any sizable omelet can be made without smashing a lot of eggs; what's more, he accepts that getting all your eggs in order (and in a kitchen hot-house like China) is not ordinarily a tea-time process.

I then raise the issue of new studies and internal revelations that seek to cut Deng down to size by raising serious questions about his true commitment to reform.

"And you don't buy the recent memoir revelation that there was less there than meets the eye?"

"He was?"

I repeat: "That there was less there than meets the eye in terms of his conversion to economic reform?"

"No, no, no. [I don't buy] that Zhao Ziyang had started it in the western part of China. Yes, Zhao Ziyang [then a very high government official, well-known reformer, and Mao critic within top leadership circles] has started some market economics in the west, but Zhao Ziyang would not have had the clout to bring the whole leadership around and say, do this. I mean, there must have been many little signs to him that if you go towards a competitive market economy, it will work better because people want to work for themselves, not for the benefit of others. When they came here [and visited us in Singapore], that clinched it."

I slip this in: "It's like you suggested to him, sure, here in Singapore, the Chinese people are doing well. But back at home there's a whole lot of Chinese people not doing well. So, what's the difference between Singapore and China? It's the system, right?"

Lee, nodding vigorously in agreement while still coughing: "As he opened up, he saved China."

That is a breathtaking encomium to think about it: *one man saved China.* LKY stops here and executes a body movement that is so expressive and typical of him. I've seen it many times. It conveys something of a total physical and mental commitment to getting his answer exactly right. He takes your question, internalizes it, pivots 45 degrees away from you, kind of runs it up and down his internal body computer, then pivots back at you in the reverse 45-degree direction, and, with his hands out and up, like a conductor about to cue the orchestra, presents his view.

His thinking about China is based on two factors. One is

his pragmatism: China exists and what are we going to do about it? The second is that China is Chinese, which on the whole he thinks a good thing. LKY is anything but pro-communist, to say the least; but anyone who would wish gargantuan China and its 1.4 billion people a condemnation to continual disaster, disease and dissolution is either evil or insane. And anyone who would have underestimated Deng, that little chain-smoking midget of a man, was to be proven as wrong as anyone could be.

> I would say the greatest was Deng Xiaoping. At his age, to admit that he was wrong ... you need a great man to do that and to convince or override his Old Guard colleagues and say, now we go this different way.

Lee goes on, in an undertone of almost palpable anger: "At first he was condemned by the West." Deng wanted to reform the country without undermining order, which might risk another monumental Cultural Revolution-like catastrophe. "They would have preferred him to be a Gorbachev and then see that China is in ruins." He laughs. "And so then they patronized Deng," he adds, shaking his head wearily.

Lee appreciates the late Deng not only as the strong leader of a sprawling country almost impossible to lead, but also as an historic Chinese leader whose rule began the corrective process of reversing European humiliation. Strong Chinese rule, under this vision, is not only an inevitability but also a necessity. In any positive

Darwinian progression, the Chinese civilization would naturally rise to the top, along with other more capable races.

As that process proceeds in accordance with some historical rhyme and rhythm, the United States and the People's Republic of China are forced to co-exist as sometimes-cooperating, sometimes-competing centers of gravity planted in the ground of (one dearly hopes) planetary stability. The latter half of the 21st century may well prove to be Asia's time for dominance, as the 19th was the European Century. But that's not going to evolve overnight by any means, and for the foreseeable future, the visionary quality and leadership capabilities of the United States will be central to world affairs, as of course they were during the last century, the well-named American one.

So, Lee worries as much about the top dogs in America as in China. As empathetic, if not chauvinistic, as Lee is about the Chinese surge, he is not one to assume America is finished anytime soon. A great admirer of entrepreneurial Americans, especially when they are at their most pragmatic and decent, he probably cares who is president at any one time as much, if not more, than the average American.

I ask: "So who is the greatest United States president that you've seen?"

"That I have *seen*?"

"Yeah. To whom you were close enough to make an assessment."

His answer will surprise very many Americans.

"But for the misfortune of Watergate, I would say Richard Nixon. He had a realistic view of the world. He was a great analyst, realistic, but also a tactician to get things done. But this need with wanting to know everything and to make sure he got re-elected became obsessive. And, too, I think he was ill served by his two aides. What were they called?"

"Haldeman and Ehrlichman?"

"Yeah. I mean, they should have said, forget it, makes no difference." But Nixon had to discover every single thing his political opponents were up to.

I say: "President Nixon ultimately didn't have the character to get out of his own way."

"No, he need not have done that. He was bound to win anyway."

LKY wasn't the only Asian leader sorry to observe Nixon's unceremonious abdication from Washington—in a helicopter. If you poll the Asian elite of his generation, Nixon would probably be no worse than near the top of the list of American presidents who've impacted Asia positively. Especially among non-communist Asian leaders, the American war in Vietnam was much less unpopular than with the U.S. public.

The opening to China, as preliminary as it was, continues to

> But for the misfortune of Watergate, I would say Richard Nixon. He had a realistic view of the world. He was a great analyst, realistic, but also a tactician to get things done.

be viewed by many in Asia as an historical master stroke.

The main motive of Nixon and Kissinger was not to cater to Asian priorities or to be cool cats with China, to be sure, but to discomfort the Soviet Union as much as possible. But the collateral benefit was enormous: to open up a new chapter in Washington-Beijing relations.

Nixon first visited with LKY in 1967, before the California congressman (and once-defeated presidential candidate) went to the White House on his second try. The career Republican—and, it needs to be noted, career communist critic—trolled around the world to beef up his international portfolio (that is, to seem more like a statesman to the American voter). In particular, Harvard Professor Henry Kissinger, who was to become Nixon's national security advisor and then secretary of state, had recommended the Singapore stop.

I ask LKY to look back through the decades: "I mean, what strikes me in your written memoirs about Nixon is, according to you, how much he listened to you."

"Yes, of course."

Well, modesty probably isn't my strongest suit, either.

I say: "But Americans, of course, are not known necessarily as being good listeners."

"He not only listened, he took notes."

"That's what I'm doing!"

He brushed off the pale effort at humor like old lint: "No, he asked me about Mao. So, I gave him a graphic assessment of what

I thought Mao was doing. I said that Mao is painting on a mosaic with 5,000 years of history behind the mosaic. He's painting his picture on it. The rains will come. What he's said will be washed away, what's been settled for 5,000 years will remain. This is Confucius."

That was a striking image: that the DNA of the culture remains far more deeply embedded than some modern ideological flimflam.

Me asking: "You think they'll ever take that gosh-awful picture [of Mao] down in Tiananmen?"

"Eventually, but not now. I mean, that's the present ruling elite's label of legitimacy. He freed China from feudalism."

In 1969, at the White House, LKY met with Nixon a second time. The father of modern Singapore reiterated his view that the feral Cultural Revolution would someday peter out, as would many of Mao's ill-conceived 'campaigns' to transform China, but that the U.S. intervention in Vietnam must not end too quickly.

Note that Nixon and Kissinger endured fierce domestic criticism for the turtle-pace of their reluctant withdrawal from Vietnam; but, according to Lee's advice at the time, slowing it down was exactly the way to go. One wonders about the enormity of the impression of Lee's views on Nixon and Kissinger!

Lee supported a policy that was known as Vietnamization— equipping the anti-communist Vietnamese to fight the communists themselves. Lee sincerely believed that an abrupt U.S. forces pullout would have emboldened the Vietnamese communists, their allies and their sympathizers to knock over one Southeast Asian country after another like, well, wavering dominos. Lee is second to no one I know in his view that the Marxist-Leninist is first and foremost interested in seizing and keeping power. Everything else (economic development, social justice) is much further from the heart.

Note that Kissinger's secret visit to Beijing in 1971 to prepare for Nixon's secret visit in 1972 was not by any means the sole reason for Asia's high regard for the former Harvard professor. It was also his well-articulated sense of world political dynamics as being so deeply rooted in history and culture that significant change does not come easily, and often arrives convulsively. In this regard the Kissinger mind-set seemed more Asian than American.

"And from the standpoint of secretary of state, I take it that you're a fan of Kissinger?"

"Sorry?" I catch him fiddling with the heat pad again.

"You're a fan of Kissinger, right?"

"Yes," and then he added another name of a Republican president's secretary of state—George Shultz: "They're both stable, they're comprehensive in their approach. Kissinger has the advantage of being more expressive with words. George Shultz hasn't quite got the same literary style. He's very precise. So, he hasn't got the free-flowing, colorful, contrapuntal balance of Kissinger's German balanced, rounded, long phrases."

Me saying: "Well, not only that, but someone who knows George well says that George is so parsimonious with words that when he's talking, you almost get the feeling that he feels he has to part with $5 out of his own pocket for every extra word he uses."

But LKY wasn't buying that oft-told jibe about Shultz.

By contrast, Clinton's secretaries of state never struck LKY as anything very special. The question is pushed not to make the case that, were he an American he'd be a Republican rather than a Democrat. Rather, it is aimed at showing the degree to which he is comfortable appraising 'foreign talent', and the extent to which Singapore's fortunes ride on the abilities of the U.S. superpower elite to perform at a high level.

I tease this out: "Basically in foreign policy, Clinton wasn't that strong, was he?"

"Well, Warren Christopher was not much. Then Madeleine Albright was not better."

"She was worse?"

"She did not have the historical depth of Henry Kissinger."

I say: "In public Christopher was probably bland, but at least he was very competent, and then, let's see who else we've had? Then Bush had, as you would say, there was Cheney and Rumsfeld, really running it. Condi was..."

"And Colin Powell was pushed aside."

He said it with sadness. LKY cares about the caliber of the elites running the top countries because he believes the priorities, conduct and decisions of the global elite are essential to securing a better future. Singapore without its governing elite would not be where it is today. Irrational democracies sometimes do little more than legitimize mob rule or policy preferences, not the surest route to quality governance; even at their best, they are hard put, in his view, to compete with truly qualified, non-corrupt and well-motivated elites.

Me asking: "Speaking of which, who's the worst American president you had seen up close?"

"Carter. He's a good God-fearing man. When you are the president of America to ruminate at Camp David, then come down to say Americans were in deep difficulties…"

"The infamous malaise speech in 1979."

"No, your job as a leader is to inspire and to galvanize, not to share your distraught thoughts. You make your people dispirited." For Lee, serious, competent governance requires making difficult policy choices and seeing them through to effect, even against strong opposition and the tide of public opinion.

"Is the second worst that you've seen Bush Jr., George W?"

"I would not put him the second worst. I would say Bush Jr. had melancholy advisers."

Interesting choice of word—melancholy.

Then LKY throws out a really fine insight: "Bush Jr. knew he didn't have much experience. It is virtue to know yourself."

I mention that, prior to the Bush Jr. years, many Americans had a high view of Cheney, with his extensive experience in Congress and the Executive.

He nods—and wishes not to add anything more there. He has just zipped up his mouth!

I mention the 41st president of the United States, 43rd's father.

"He was a balanced, thoughtful man. Unfortunately he had this thyroid problem during his re-election campaign and showed he had lost energy. Had he not been lethargic, he could have won. He had governed well; he had fought the first Iraq War well. The economic downturn couldn't be helped."

> **No, your job as a leader is to inspire and to galvanize, not to share your distraught thoughts. You make your people dispirited.**

I jab in: "He also ran up against a phenomenal domestic politician, Bill Clinton."

"No, had he not lost his energy, he would have won."

I suggest again: "Well, the economy seemed to be tanking then." Americans will well remember the Clinton campaign-staff motivational mantra in running against the senior Bush: "It's the economy, stupid."

"The economic downturn couldn't be helped."

I let that go, not agreeing—and he knew that I doubted his view—then saying: "Interesting. Well, what *do* you think of Clinton?"

"Very clever man, very political, likeable fellow because he's got that outgoing personality."

"Yeah, terrific personality."

"When he talks to you, you are the most important person in the world. But I think, it's generally true, he breaks the rules."

"Too much American freedom?"

"Well, in his case, it's partly his character. I don't know. I mean, he had a difficult childhood and so on, so forth."

I let the psychoanalysis go. But I am struck by two things.

One is his clinical analysis of the vaunted Clinton charm. It is clear that life had somehow immunized him to it. Legend has it that former China President Jiang Zemin also was immune to Clinton's charm offensives, which, allegedly, he found quite offensive. But other than Zemin and LKY, there is only one other major world political figure publicly known to have found nothing whatsoever charming about the Arkansas charm-machine. That was George W. Bush, his successor.

> I would say Bush Jr. had melancholy advisers.... [He] knew he didn't have much experience. It is virtue to know yourself.

Question: so, besides their Clinton immunology, what in the world do LKY, Zemin and Bush Jr. have in common?

Think about it.

The other notable edge to Lee's views is his complete contempt for a ruler who would be brought down by misconduct with a woman. His own public conduct with—and attitude about—women is evidently without controversy. There has never been a breath of scandal. His own writings reveal a near-worship toward his mother, and infinite love for his wife of many decades. His government's social, political and economic policies have always forcefully favored equality of opportunity and achievement. They have created a women's professional class that never existed on the island 50 years ago. It will take another generation or so, perhaps, for that equality to reach the very tip of the top of Singapore; but increasingly Singaporean women are in the driver's seat. Unlike affirmative-action apologists, LKY would never rush women into top positions just for appearance's sake; but he fully expects women to be well-represented in the next generation of Singapore leaders.

The motive was not so much ideology as practicality. LKY's government was able to double the size of its (relatively tiny) adult workforce simply by enforcing policies to eliminate discriminations that hold women back. By the 80s and 90s, Singaporean women comprised world-class achievers in many professional fields. They were so capable and outstanding that they sometimes scared away potential suitors—Singaporean Chinese men who were culturally unprepared to relate to their partners as flat-out, even-up socio-economic equals.

LKY once confided to me that he secretly admired the Japanese for slowing down this advance in order to maintain cultural continuity. There are a number of reasons why Singapore now has one of the lowest birth rates in Asia, but one of them is this: some powerhouse women scare the living daylights out of some Singaporean men. At the same time, Japan's economy, on idle for two decades now, might have done better had women been more dynamically integrated in the workforce.

Singapore felt it had no choice. In the mid-60s, when it was forced out of a two-year trial federation with Malaysia, it was suddenly on its own—sink or swim. And so, the otherwise conservative Confucian culture didn't have the luxury of going Japanese-slow on anything. In addition, the social and economic liberation of women (Chinese and family-oriented Confucian culture notwithstanding) fit well within Lee's merit-driven instincts.

So I push on: "Well, luck of the draw, but the reason I'm asking these questions is not only because I'm interested in what you actually think, but also just look at the American system and our allegedly terrific system of democracy. Have we produced the best?

"Let me just look at Singapore. You used to have Kishore Mahbubani at the UN, and he was terrific. Before that, you had Tommy Koh, and he was terrific. Your long-running lady diplomat, Chan Heng Chee, in Washington, is terrific. I mean, they've all punched above their weight. I'm a fan of George Yeo, your foreign minister, and I don't know the rest of your camp, but you have some terrific people.

"I mean, Charlene Barshefsky [Clinton's trade adviser] used to tell me that when you go to these international trade conferences and it would be like two in the morning and somebody will say, what's the precedent for X or Y, and then everyone would turn to the Singapore delegation for the answer, because it was always the best prepared delegation. I mean, here's a system that produces that quality and we just produce…"

He smiles, obviously proud of the international teams Singapore puts out for people to see: "Well, that's the nature of your political appointments. You know, you've got to appoint people who have donated to the campaign, or to re-election ... appoint people you're obliged to. Where you have a free hand and appoint the most competent, then it's different."

"That's consistent with your theme, it seems to me, of the limitations of democracy?"

He answers cautiously, for this is obviously sensitive ground: "Well, I think the presidential system is less likely to produce good government than a parliamentary system. In the presidential system, your personal appearance on TV is decisive, whereas in a parliamentary system, the prime minister, before he becomes the prime minister, has been a member of parliament, and probably a minister, and in Britain the people have sized you up over a period of time, you know, and they have come to certain conclusions as to what kind of a person you are, what kind of depth you have, what kind of sincerity you have in what you say.

"So, the party then chooses the man most likely to lead them to victory the next time round. They choose the man with the most political weight and also the administrative capacity to get his policies implemented so that after five years, they can win again. Your presidents, I mean, like Jimmy Carter ... my name is Jimmy Carter, I'm a peanut farmer, I'm running for president. The next thing you know, he was the president!"

"We had a peanut as president, right?"

"I mean, my first meeting with him was a shock, you know?"

"Why?"

"He did me the favor of seeing me within a month after taking office. So, he's quite new. His aides must have said he [this Singapore guy] is worth seeing. It was a five-minute photo ops … at the mantlepiece, photo ops. It was all choreographed. Then photographers out, seven minutes tête-à-tête, then full meeting. What did he raise? … Why do you want this improved Hawk? I said, what's that? 'Improved Hawk, it's an improved version of the surface-to-air missile.' I said, because it's an advance on what we have. [I guffaw loudly at this.] He said, it's high technology, do you need it? I said, we think we do, but if you have any trouble at all, I'd get it from the British. I said, it's not a matter of life and death.

"So, we went through the main meeting, one hour, the balance of one hour, and he had a laundry list and he went through all the laundry list, all the irrelevant small things. Whereas I've been discussing with Nixon and with Ford; Ford was really Henry Kissinger running the [foreign-policy] show, all the big issues in East Asia, where is it heading, how is it going, where is Southeast Asia going to fit in all this?"

LKY sighs: "I left bemused, and he gave me a book, his campaign book called *Why Not The Best?* So, I went back to the hotel. I said, let's find out what he's like. I was astounded. He recounted how, as a boy, the father gave him a penny or whatever to put into the pew box, and instead of putting one in, he took a penny out. So, the father then thrashed him. I said, why does the man do that? Having done it, how does telling the world that he was a petty thief help?"

I couldn't help myself, and had to slip this in: "He also did an infamous interview with *Playboy* magazine and the famous quote was, they asked him, he was married to Rosalyn, if he ever had physical feelings for other women? And he said, 'Sometimes I have lust in my heart,' and a lot of people said, wow, that's an odd place to have lust!"

(Laughter erupts in the room; the two invisible aides are alive and breathing after all!)

LKY saying: "There's something not quite right about him. Then he went before Rickover, the admiral of the submarine fleet. So, the admiral said, what was your place in Annapolis? He said 167th or whatever. So, Rickover said, 'Why not the best?' "

The crusty, plain-speaking Rickover would say something like that, I thought to myself, then to Lee: "In a way the blunt-talking Rickover is your spiritual brother!"

He says nothing, of course.

Like the famous headstrong American tank commander, General George S. Patton (or for that matter, President Harry S. Truman), Hyman S. Rickover, the four-star admiral who invented the nuclear-powered submarine, was not for mincing words. And so his mouth would sometimes get him in trouble. But Americans, by and large, love the man of courage who says exactly what he thinks. LKY is no fan of one-man, one-vote, but in

> Well, I think the presidential system is less likely to produce good government than a parliamentary system.

America his electability quotient would be high, for the very same reasons Americans so adored Patton and Rickover.

Which rumination leads me to push the thought in another way: "Is there anyone alive today who is most like you?"

> I do not know of any person who is most like me.

A long pause here: "I do not know of any person who is most like me."

You have to laugh. He is smart. And possibly … yes … unique.

Rebel With a Cause

DO YOU BELIEVE this American journalist was shamelessly disloyal to listen silently (actually, more like guffawingly) as this foreign leader of a tiny country, without any of the burdens and responsibilities of a superpower, tore into one of our former presidents?

He utterly belittled him—an American leader who, after all, had only garnered a Nobel Peace Prize after leaving office. I mean, how many Singaporeans have won a Nobel? (Answer: zero) And so who is this LKY to be so disrespectful of the president of a country so allegedly important to Singapore and to world stability?

When LKY decides on something or someone—that such and such is unimportant, or over-rated, or not the real quality deal—you get the sense that appeals are a waste of your time and money. I tried to get former President Carter to assess the place of LKY in history, but as you noticed in the front of the book, the request was declined. I wish the former president had taken a broader view. It would be salutary for LKY to get a bit of his own medicine, as it is for all of us.

In the category of Things-He-Does-Not-Have-a-Huge-Amount-of-Respect-or-Need-for, please include near the top of the list the news media. It is believed, in the West at least, that an independent news media is essential to a political culture. Over the decades Lee has shown he believes no such thing. His government and the People's Action Party put a lid on its own media, and when they felt the foreign press was becoming too feisty, they made it more difficult for the offending news outfit to operate in Singapore.

So, to be provocative, I ask him about Singapore's own news media, often criticized in the West as supine to the government and thus intrinsically second-rate. (By the way, my own view is that, except for its obvious punch-pulling as regards the big shots at the Istana, *The Straits Times*, the country's leading daily, is a first-rate newspaper). His response is unmistakable.

He sighs, for this is not his favorite topic, especially as I am a career Western journalist: "First, the Singapore people are not deprived of any news. All magazines are available, Internet is open. What we have not allowed is for the local media to go crusading. Report factually, express your opinion in the editorial page and in letters from readers in the Forum Page. We receive many letters from the public, mostly complaints, but also some compliments and suggestions. We reply to every one of them, those that are serious. We don't own the newspapers, they are run as profitable businesses. But they are losing readers because of online news. We encourage them to report wrongdoings. That is one way for wrongdoings to surface when we miss them."

Well, that is that. His mind is made up on this. So why do we even bother to listen to this guy? But that's the fascinating issue—people do. You do. I certainly do. We all do. But why do many people want to know his views and generally listen carefully when he offers them, even though he is anything but the second coming of Thomas Jefferson on certain issues?

LKY has received honors from high-level institutions all over the world, has been often treated as a world-class senior statesman par excellence (when not being denounced as a new-age Torquemada by groups that focus almost non-contextually on issues such as human rights and capital punishment), and has climbed into—specially since stepping down as prime minister in 1990—the unofficial chair of Contemporary Asian Oracle. The well-respected American journal *Foreign Policy* even crowned him, as he turned 86, as the Asian Kissinger.

Why?

There are reasons for almost everything, as Lee would say. One is his reputation for saying pretty much what is on his mind, and you get the sense that this is one mind that is rarely blank. Another is that his intellectual independence (saying what he wants) derives in part from Singapore's position in the region and the world. Since his country depends on almost everyone for something (Malaysia for water, Indonesia for produce, the West for firearms and security, et cetera), it is wholly dependent on no one in particular.

From the U.S., for example, Lee never asked for nor accepted a dollar in formal foreign aid grants. He is not interested in being viewed as a welfare dependent on Uncle Sam. That would undermine Singapore's independence. So what praise he has for us is thus not purchased and is surely sincere; what criticisms he offers are (from his standpoint) reasoned, scientific. What's more, many people listen to him as the true Sage of Singapore, someone with decades of experience who has hung in there through thick and thin like a true warrior.

And as Asia has surged in prominence, Lee's voice has risen in parallel, as have those of some others in Singapore and elsewhere in the region. Who else are we to listen to from Asia? Only the Dalai Lama? Only China's President Hu Jintao? Some Indian guru whose name no one can pronounce?

To be sure, Singapore's high self-regard irritates its neighbors. But it is necessarily a non-threatening nation; it has never invaded anyone, and it never will, if only because it can't. It is not a nuclear power and it's hard to imagine it would ever want to be. It lurks over no one, though its defensive capabilities are no joke. This gives it a certain above-the-fray status, like some highly intellectualized and technocratic version of India back in the days when Nehru spoke with a voice that carried far beyond the Punjab.

Then there's the issue of style. Soft authoritarian or not, Lee's Cambridge diction, elite level of learning, emphasis on continued mid-career learning for himself and his elite, and focus on the big, if not philosophical, issues render his public voice distinctively instructional. Except perhaps for the very longest of his long speeches, he is always extremely interesting to listen to, and to read (his prose style is often blunt to the point of coming across as Basic Hemingway 101). His writer's voice contains recognizable elements, in various ways, of India's Nehru, the international media's David Frost, some Chinese Machiavelli and Daddy Dearest. It is an accumulated voice like no other I know of.

We chat about the importance of speechifying.

I submit: "When I was in graduate school, I took a seminar at Princeton from Ted Sorensen, who was President Kennedy's illustrious speechwriter, and he said to me this: Tom, you are a great talker and all of that, but talking is not writing."

He nods: "Yeah, talking isn't writing."

"Ted Sorensen said something like, that's really different, you've got to be more disciplined, more organized, very clear, except when you don't want to be."

"Because when you talk, you can repeat."

"And you can use body language, the atmosphere of the moment."

LKY: "When you write, you can't. The moving eye does not go back. If it has to go back, that means you've written poorly."

Me saying: "Now, if you are a good writer and a good communicator, which you are, that is a huge plus for a leader, but if you are not, it's a huge handicap for a leader."

"Well, yes, because, I mean, to be a leader, you must be able to communicate your feelings and move the other fellow. It's not just ideas, you know."

"And you don't have to be a genius. You may be, but you don't have to be. Ronald Reagan was not a genius."

"But you must move the other fellow's position."

I say: "Yeah, and be clear. After Carter, that was Reagan's great strength. He had three ideas: America is great, less government is better government, and the Soviet Union is the evil empire. End of story. That was it; that was the whole deal. But he would stay on it. He didn't change his tune every three months. Who is the great communicator of our time now in politics?"

"Today? Maybe Obama, as a fluent speaker. I am not sure whether he would produce results, but for sheer ability to put things the way he wants them, the way he feels would go down with the people, with Americans, he's got a knack for it."

It's hard to know how far that talent can carry Obama, though: "Sorensen said that too about Obama, and so, between his opinion and yours, that just about nails it for me. But, still, I have very unhappy doubts about Obama; I wonder whether he will have a second term. But leaving that aside, I remember before he was president, someone said: Obama? He is only good at giving speeches. And then Ted Sorensen weighed in and said, hey, wait a minute, that's really important for a president, to be able to communicate, to indicate direction. Don't belittle that talent."

Theodore C. Sorensen, whom I admired as a student and thereafter as a journalist, was totally devoted

> I am not sure whether he [Obama] would produce results, but for sheer ability to put things the way he wants them, the way he feels would go down with the people, with Americans, he's got a knack for it.

to John Kennedy, of course. JFK lucked out. Ted was all talent. And, like LKY, in fact, JFK as well as TS was a real writer (who in another life might have been a newspaper or newsmagazine editor), and a real thinker, sardonic and sometimes unpredictable. Kennedy, through Sorensen, it seemed to me, could often be seen searching for large, Hedgehog-like ideas; he had such a lively mind. LKY, it seems to me, is always searching for them, restlessly. But, for a number of reasons, he doesn't want to make too big a deal of it.

Passage To India

THE PUBLIC POLICY achievements of Singapore are not to be mooted simply because of its size—brains count, Lee is right. Even so, even brains aren't enough by themselves. Though more populated than Los Angeles, LKY's home country is perhaps but a third the population of Shanghai, as the late Deng Xiaoping famously suggested to him. The population of New Delhi, the capital of India, is approximately three times Singapore's. Imagine what it would be like to have to be the Big Bad Nanny over a place like India!

So I ask him that. I put it to him straight: "But could you have done it in India?"

"In India?"

"Could you have done India?"

"No."

I thought that a rather direct answer: "But why?"

"It's an established ancient civilization. Nehru and Gandhi had a chance because of their enormous prestige, but they couldn't break the caste system. They could not break the habits."

Notice he didn't mention the size-of-population issue.

To LKY an inherited culture is sort of like a country's DNA.

To change it almost requires laser surgery. Cultures that evolve to changes in circumstances and challenges can thrive; those that do not, fall behind. In a famous and influential 1994 interview with Fareed Zakaria in *Foreign Affairs*, the semi-official journal of the U.S. foreign-policy establishment, Lee spelled out his Toynbee-esque view that culture is destiny. That's why he often admonishes critics to understand a country's 'starting place'.

So I venture this: "But the great Nehru added to the problem of India because he was stuck on an idea: Soviet central planning!"

"Yeah, he was."

"But you would have dropped that in three months?"

He nods, as if sure: "You see, he was stuck on big ideas. He went for ideas. I chase ideas provided they work. When they don't work, I say, look, this idea maybe sounds bright, but let's try something that works. So we try something that works, let's get it going."

If you believe in numbers as a fully satisfying measurement of true achievement, Singapore under Lee and his successors has been using ideas that work for decades. Consider that in 2008, the per capita income of India was US$2,900, number 167 in the world. But Singapore's was US$51,600, eighth in the world. The U.S. number—and this surprised me—was but tenth, at US$47,500. Over the decades Singapore put a lot of policy stuff into successful motion.

I say: "Your aide and I were talking about the glorious gardens here in Istana, and looking at them as little laboratories. You bring some little plant in and if it dies, you don't try to plant them elsewhere in the country, right? Didn't work, don't do it. But Nehru, was he someone who was too much of a Hedgehog, perhaps stuck on big ideas?"

LKY tilts his head slightly downward: "I don't know whether he is a Hedgehog, but he is a man who plays with ideas, you know, 'Non-Aligned Third World', not committed to either side when, in fact, he was committed to the Soviet side in the end, because you need advanced-technology weaponry, and so he chose to criticize America. He didn't get on with John Kennedy; you remember the famous interchange: Kennedy showed him how the wealthy lived in America, grand buildings, et cetera, and Nehru was unimpressed. I mean, I would not have been un-impressed! So, he's a different man, his mental make-up. So, he writes books, he writes beautiful books. He's an anti-colonialist, he's a freedom fighter, but what do you do with freedom? What is it that your people want?"

This is a key cry with LKY. *What do people really want?*

He continues: "Gandhi's idea was to give them back the village, the spinning wheel. Well, I mean, that's going to get you nowhere in this Industrial Age."

But this is getting us somewhere: "You say at one point, what do people want? Do they want food on the table, a car, a home, or they want the right to write any editorial in a newspaper? And then you say, I know what they want. You say they want reality, not concepts. That's your view. But, even so, Nehru was a great man."

India today is increasingly important to Lee's Singapore. Nobody in the region wants to bet everything on China. He picks through foreign policy options the way a NASCAR driver plots out an upcoming race. The main concern is not what happens if everything goes right, but what the options are at any given point when things go wrong (as sometimes they do). If Singapore puts all its diplomatic chips on giant China, which then turns angrily on its smallest neighbors (or internally implodes, which has happened before, and could happen again—let's face it), what is its way out of the box it put itself in? Lee knows that without India actively involved in Southeast Asia, ASEAN alone cannot hope to stand against China on any important issue.

> I chase ideas provided they work. When they don't work, I say, look, this idea maybe sounds bright, but let's try something that works.

Lee shrugs as we review all this geopolitical landscape. Without exchanging a word, we accept that China will probably hold to 'peaceful rising', in Beijing's stilted mantra. Or that view could prove naïve and it might wake up one day and follow in the footsteps of any number of giants in history and start eating up tiny neighbors.

This is where India might come in handy. It's not hard to follow Lee's crisp logic.

"Who is the counterweight? Japan cannot be the counterweight. It has not got enough bodies. Together Japan and America, yes, can be a counterweight, economically and physically, and militarily, but who is the X counterweight within Asia, because

America may, in 100, 200 years, become less able to dominate Asia. But the Indians are here for keeps."

The former prime minister explains the hedging strategy: "So, we developed relations with India. Prime Minister Manmohan Singh [India's brainy prime minister] and I have been trying to get Indians into [the political community of] Southeast Asia for decades, from Mrs. Indira Gandhi onwards, but they were always too preoccupied with Pakistan. So, Manmohan Singh, as finance minister, faced his problems and his kitty was running very low, foreign exchange…"

"You mean in the 1990s?"

"Yes. So, he changed economic strategy, and came here, together with his trade minister, who is now home minister, Chidambaram, and says, will you endorse this [such-and-such a finance program] because if we endorse it, it becomes more credible. So, I said, yes, of course. So, we developed that relationship and we gradually brought them into ASEAN as a dialogue partner on equal terms with China. Then for the East Asia Summit, which the Chinese were going to dominate, we brought the Indians and the Australians and the New Zealanders for balance. So, they know that we are their friends."

Returning to the Indians, he expresses satisfaction at Singapore's steady development of a solid bilateral relationship to offset a possible (if so far only theoretical) unpleasant China syndrome. But this get-it-done man, even in his mid-eighties, hasn't slowed down enough to tolerate one of India's least endearing traits: a bureaucracy that moves with the approximate speed of a backlash of taffy.

"So, we've got access to them," he nearly groans, "but unfortunately, their bureaucracy is so slow."

"Yeah, it's amazing."

"So many things we could do with them are not being done."

I don't mention it to LKY, but one difference between his country and India is that for the former, which is a relatively progressive society, the default position for trying anything new seems to have been a 'yes'. But for India, which is relatively traditional, the default appears to remain a 'no'.

Then I slip into the role of agent provocateur, saying sarcastically: "But India's a democracy."

"So?"

This—Occidental fans of the Orient—was not 'so' as in 'ah so'. It was 'so' as in 'so what?' I am telling you, dear reader, Thomas Jefferson does not live in the Istana. Neither (for you political philosopher fans) does John Rawls. So who does? My answer comes later.

If morally or religiously you believe that one-man, one-vote is axiomatically the correct system, are you prepared to pay a 'democracy tax'? Even in the best run of them, you have to incur a substantial inefficiency (and, unusually, corruption) deficit. This is not to suggest that a suffocating bureaucracy is the inevitable concomitant of a democratic system: to be sure, sludge-filled bureaucracies are scarcely the monopoly of democracies; they can breed like cancer in autocracies just as pathologically.

India's bureaucracy, though, is pretty much the stuff of legend; what's amazing is that democratically elected figures like Manmohan Singh manage to achieve as much as they do in the face of a system that, culturally and dynamically, has more respect for the past than the future.

We go on: "So, now fast forward, the next decade, after he visited you, he then becomes prime minister. Is he just a puppet?"

Lee saying: "He is there on the support of Mrs. Sonia Gandhi but, no, no, he is not a puppet. When Sonia Gandhi hesitated about the very big nuclear deal with America, he said, I will resign if you don't support it. So, she supported him."

"And he got it." India is receiving oodles of nuclear technology from Uncle Sam.

"And he got it and that was a good move."

"Is it a good move for America too, do you think?" Many Americans opposed it because of blanket opposition to the spread of nuclear technology. You might even call the opponents the ayatollahs of nuclear proliferation doctrine.

"Yes, surely." Lee is not one for doctrine. Or for ayatollahs, especially of the academic kind.

"So, that is where you put pragmatics over ideology?"

"Yes, of course."

Guess Who's
Coming To Dinner?

SURVIVAL.

Lee's vision of geopolitical stability would require, for starters, an adult working relationship among great powers. Any thrust for hegemony by any one power is inherently disturbing and destabilizing. It is the moral as well as politically realistic position for all to oppose such a buildup by one power alone.

Even if Singapore were not the little bird pecking away on the top of the hippo to survive, but were itself one of the hippos, his vision and instinct would not change. Even in the mind of an alleged 'soft authoritarian', there have to be limits on the freedom of the strongest, as of course they burden the weakest.

Survival. LKY himself is quite the survivor. In an environment of utter comfort bereft of challenge, he would shrink psychologically to a more normal dimension of political actor. In the reality of his own mind, he sees existential challenges everywhere. He is still unconvinced that mainly Muslim Malaysia is no longer a military threat to 76 percent Chinese Singapore.

As he puts it to me: "Both our northern and southern neighbors are much larger than us. Both have Muslim majorities and are differently organized. Both have not completely accepted their ethnic Chinese citizens. This accentuates the religious and cultural divide, and a subconscious sense of being a nut in a nutcracker."

Paranoid?

Or prudent?

Threats are everywhere. He has seen off engineers to Holland to study the science of dike building in the event the pace of global warming quickens and a rising sea level threatens Singapore's reclaimed land. He most admires those who take destiny in their hands rather than cower in indecisiveness. He admires no one more than the Israelis for their hard-scrabble, high-IQ survivalism.

I look up from my yellow pad on which are scribbled topics I want at least to touch on before the clock runs out: "There's a line in your autobiography that I just want to have a little fun with if you would. You talked about 'every society has a small percentage that's exceptionally able. These people are like the philosopher-kings of old. They will have to be thrown up through a meritocratic process or be actively sought out to lead. Doing so helps raise the lot of all society far more than pretending that all men are equally capable or talented.' Then at one point, you said, and I found this hilarious: 'I'm not as smart as an Israeli.' "

"Yeah, that's right."

"Whatever do you mean by that?"

He turned to stare at me, an eyebrow almost raised, as if the point were obvious: "The Israelis are very smart."

"Why?"

He searches his memory for a story: "I asked a Bank of America president in 1990 or something, why are the Jews so smart? And he gave me a book, his own copy, well-thumbed. So—I had it bound up because it might come apart; I think I've still got it somewhere—I read it through, small book. And, well, it didn't go into the pogroms and how the stupid people, the slow and the half-witted, were destroyed and the bright ones survived. He emphasized how the good genes multiplied. He said the rabbi in any Jewish society was often the most intelligent and well-read, most learned of all because he's got to know Hebrew, he's got to know the Talmud, he's got to know various languages and so on. So, the rabbi's children are much sought-after by successful Jews to bring the good genes into the family. That's how they multiply, the bright ones multiply. That sums it up."

I say: "And whereas in the Catholic Church, the priests will destroy that [by not procreating] and so the Church's kids are getting dumber."

"And the priests are thinning out to nothingness now. That's right."

LKY adheres to the almost mechanistic logic of eugenics and negative eugenics the way the 'scientific' baseball manager relies on statistics of home runs and strikeouts to make game decisions. If such and such a batter has a .200 lifetime average against left-handed pitchers, that batter will not likely be permitted to come to the plate late in a close game against a left-handed pitcher. Similarly, smart couples are more likely to produce smart children than couples that are less smart (however measured). The problem for Singapore (and others in Asia, including Hong Kong and Japan) is that more and more smart couples are having fewer and fewer children. Under the *dis*-eugenics hypothesis, this means each successive generation becomes less smart, like a systematically shrinking Catholic-priest population.

Lee's solution for his country's dilemma is to open doors to foreigners who want to become Singaporean, but not to all outsiders—only to the educated professionals, the achievers, the brains, the elite. In almost any democracy, such thoughts by a leader would get him into a boil of trouble. LKY says that he does not worry much about being politically correct. If a given proposition is true and germane to good governance, it is a betrayal of trust to act as if such a truth doesn't exist. Burying it under the sawdust of political correctness is to lay a land mine for yourself. If a certain ethnic or racial group is overwhelmingly disadvantaged regarding this or that, ignoring that reality, by not treating it, only perpetuates the negative consequences of the disadvantage.

A merit-based system advantages everyone, the less able included, by having governance driven by the best. Suggesting that everyone is equal or that the exceptionally able population is anything but a small percentage of the whole is, in his view, arrant foolishness and, at worst, an evil deception. Purely democratic systems which are not strictly meritocratic tend to elevate mediocrity. The honest, courageous leader—or contemporary 'prince'—will not hesitate to tell the truth publicly and act on it. Yes, sometimes people's feelings will get hurt.

Political systems vary by the terrain. Israel is basically a Western-style democracy, and the Catholic Church is not. Neither is China. All three dominions in one way or the other, at given times, have been successful. But democracy ideologues will not be happy until everyone is a democracy. China is often urged by the West to open up and democratize, even overnight.

I say, trying to cover a lot of territory quickly: "In 1999, in Beijing, Clinton said bluntly to China's President Jiang Zemin, during a memorable joint public TV appearance, that the Chinese government's thinking about how to govern was on the wrong side of history. Is it?"

"They never thought so then, they even less so think so now."

"But what do you think?"

"No, I didn't think so then and I don't think so now. I think their way has kept China together and they are making progress, but they're going to face many problems along the road. Technology is going to make their system of governance obsolete. By 2030, 70 percent or maybe 75 percent of their people will be in cities, small towns, big towns, mega big towns. They're going to have cell phones, Internet, satellite TV. They're going to be well-informed; they can organize themselves. You can't govern them the way you're governing them now where you just placate and they monitor a few people because the numbers will be so large. They know this and they don't know where they will end up, but they believe step by step, as the situation changes, they adapt, they change, they can remain in control and they co-opt the bright people and the activists into their party. It's no longer a communist party. It is a party of all those who will make China great and strong. That's all."

Me adding: "But the wrong side of history point, it goes back to the Francis Fukuyama book, *The End of History*, and not only was he wrong in the sense that unpredictable history keeps rolling on whether we like it or not, but maybe our cherished democratic system in America is the exception that doesn't prove the rule. In other words, that other forms of governance are going to be more thematic in the future."

LKY adds: "I do not believe that one-man, one-vote, in either the U.S. format or the British format or the French format, is the final position. I mean, human society will change over the years with technology, with free travel. The demographics of countries are changing with mixtures of population.

"What will be the end result? I don't know. I mean, what will be the future of the U.S. to begin with? The Chinese have projected it and they are fairly confident. They see themselves as relatively homogenous. Yes, they'll absorb a few more foreigners along the coastal cities, but they're likely to remain, as today, 90 percent Han. In fifty years' time, at the most, another 10 percent non-Han, mixed; 80 percent Han. By comparison, they see the U.S. and their migration patterns. By 2050, the Hispanics will overtake the Anglo-Saxons. So, either you change their culture or they change you, and I do not believe you can change their culture."

Lee continues, at breakneck speed now: "I mean, you look at Latin America. You might change the culture of a few whom you now appoint. Those Hispanics that Obama has appointed to the cabinet or Clinton appointed to the cabinet or George Bush appointed to the cabinet, those are exceptional Hispanics, but the total Hispanic culture will remain what it is. So, you will lose your dynamism, and if you continue with one-man, one-vote, they will set the agenda because they are the majority."

> I do not believe that one-man, one-vote, in either the U.S. format or the British format or the French format, is the final position. I mean, human society will change over the years...

I think it is fair to say that Lee would not win any election in any district dominated by Latinos, not to mention by Uighurs or Sinhalese. Here, the deeply embedded American penchant for optimism might come in handy for dealing with what is probably inevitable: continuing waves of immigration into a country whose spectacular success has been built on the brains, as well as the backs, of immigrants, few of whom came here with PhDs, MDs or law degrees. But their kids and then their kids have them in droves.

Lee of Arabia

NEAR THE OPENING of *Lawrence of Arabia*, the epic film by Sir David Lean, a very elderly Sir Lawrence hops onto his motorbike for an early morning spin. Determined and uncaring as a teenager, he slams on the accelerator and roars down the country road like the proverbial bat out of hell. This is the end of his life, but the beginning of the film. An overnight storm has felled a tree across the road that on this fateful morning is to take Lawrence to his last violent run-in: a deadly collision with a stone wall.

Perhaps this biker or race car imagery works as reasonably well for Harry as for Lawrence, with one footnote: LKY, unlike Lawrence, always worries about potential disaster.

Driver Lee has always pushed the Singapore accelerator as fast as he reasonably can, though all the time worrying about an accident or upset. Like a seasoned race-car driver at Le Mans, he worries not what he will do to win the race as much as what he will do to save the day if the unexpected were suddenly to happen, as it often does.

LKY is very good at worrying. He might agree that it's one of his best talents. He was worrying about the Islamic world long before September 11, 2001. That was the date when Americans, gliding without a care in the world along the country road, smashed into their stone wall.

It's no surprise that LKY has given the Islamic challenge much thought. In addition to his deep-seated aversion to surprises, he does live in a country with sprawling Indonesia all but surrounding it—and with the rest of the mostly Muslim Malaysian peninsula above it. This is where very many Muslims live. Indonesia is home to more Muslims than any other country. (You may be surprised, though, that India, usually viewed as a Hindu culture, has the globe's second largest concentration, with neighboring Pakistan third.)

So I suggest that the resurgence of the Islamic world could also have a dramatic effect on the world agenda, not just the American one. The late Samuel Huntington, a storied Harvard professor, coined the phrase 'The Clash of Civilizations' to title his most famous book. Huntington was fascinated by LKY's Singapore, but once predicted that the country would not survive in its present, uncorrupted form upon Lee's departure from earth. Huntington was to change that view after a wide-ranging conversation, perhaps not unlike this one, with Lee.

Lee recalls vividly: "We used to meet at the Asia Society and so on, he came here and I went there; and one day, he sent me a piece he was writing in the *Foreign Affairs* called the 'Clash of Civilizations'. Then I saw him and I said, look, I agree with you only where the Muslims are concerned, only there. I should have written it in a piece or in a letter to him, my thought turned out prophetic.

I said, Hinduism, Chinese Confucianism or Communism, Japanese Shintoism, they are secular really. They know that to progress, you must master science and technology, and that's where they are going to compete with you in the end. But the Muslims believe that if they mastered the Quran and they are prepared to do all that Muhammad has prescribed, they will succeed. So, we can expect trouble from them and so, it happened."

"And here we are today."

"Yeah. Why did I come to that conclusion? Because I saw the Malays with whom I went to school; they were quite eclectic and secular during British times."

I am puzzled: "Quite what?"

"*Eclectic.* You know, I will eat pork, [they will eat] whatever they eat, their halal food, and, in college, we'll sit down the same table. Women will not have scarves and so on. But with the rise of oil money, the Saudis and others invited them to conferences and said, look, yours is a diluted voice of Islam. We are the gold standard, pray five times a day, do that, women should not show their limbs, cover up to the sleeves and the ankles, and gradually, now you see so many of the women with headscarves. Are you mad?"

I look at Lee and we both cannot help chortling. We mean no disrespect to any religion. Still, any religion that requires you to dress like Eskimos in all kinds of weather, including dense humid tropical heat, perhaps might merit a sartorial as well as ecclesiastical review by common sense.

He continues: "So, then one day, the prime minister of

Mauritius comes by on his way to Australia for some conference. He said, are your Malays here in Singapore, are your Muslims becoming different? So, [Senior Minister] Goh Chok Tong says, why do you ask? He says, our Mus [they call them Mus for Muslims] have suddenly changed. The Saudis have built a mosque, beautiful mosque, and sent them preachers. Now, they have segregated themselves."

Lee rolls his black eyes: "And I was listening to BBC, the reporter saying that was happening in Africa too. So, I see the oil money and the [hard-core] Wahabis rallying a Muslim world to their side. Now, in the years before the oil boom, when you go on a Haj, you go to a Third World country. Now, you go on a Haj, you are in a super First World country; you see brand-new great buildings, motorways, air-conditioned, everything. So, they are overwhelmed by this. It's like, if you behave like a proper Muslim, Allah will give you oil!"

"So they were right all along!"

"Yeah! Now, you see, Islam came to Southeast Asia not by conquest but by traders from Yemen, and because it came with sailing ships, sailing boats, there was distance and, therefore, it developed in a different, milder way, especially in Indonesia where they had an under-layer of animism, Javanese superstition, Hinduism, Buddhism. So, even today, I believe the average Javanese is less prone to extremism. So, the people in Indonesia who are pushing a harder view are Arabs, of Arab descent, like Abu Bakar Bashir, who is a pure Arab."

I interjected: "You mean the reputed ideological godfather of Jemaah Islamiyah, the militant Islamic movement based in Indonesia, the group that would like to conflate Indonesia, Malaysia, southern Islamic Philippines, Brunei and even Singapore into one vast orthodox Islamic state?"

Lee nods: "Of course, they have succeeded in getting the poor Javanese to follow them and sacrifice themselves."

Such good friends, Saudi Arabia and the United States: "So, instead of invading Iraq, we should have invaded Saudi Arabia?"

Sometimes my so-called interviewing technique involves deliberately absurd suggestions.

"No way!"

"But 10, 15, 25 years from now, this Islam thing, a bigger problem or is it going to be a lesser problem?"

"Depends on what happens in the oil states, particularly Saudi Arabia. Especially if Saudi Arabia wants to modernize, which I think some of the princes want to do, like Prince Abdullah now, although he's going about it slowly and he is an old man. So, it depends on who succeeds him. Then they've got to move away from this compact by which they plead with the Wahabis: you support my royal family and I will give you the resources to spread your Wahabism. So, now, women cannot drive cars, et cetera, but behind these high walls of all the royal princes and princesses, they take off their veils and put on their Parisian clothes; and the men got the bars and clubs to go to and so on. I mean, it's a hypocritical society. So, for weekends, they go to Dubai."

Lee is clearly no fan of this world, but has respect for cosmopolitan Muslims, especially Abdullah: "He's now opened a King Abdullah University for Science and Technology, and within that university, all rules are off. Women can study with men, no scarves, you can drink what you like, et cetera, but the moment you leave, you've got to comply. If that side succeeds in gathering momentum, then I think Saudi Arabia will change, but if they go back to, if they regress and you get a younger generation of princes keeping up the same bargain with the Wahabis, I don't know what will happen."

"So, if there is one key to this 'clash of civilizations' business, it's Saudi Arabia?"

"Yes, and they have the oil. So, are you going to invade and take over the oil?"

I joke: "Go back to bicycles!"

"And then, you cannot fly to Singapore anymore!"

"On Singapore Airlines!"

"Well, of course."

Years of Living Dangerously
(With Indonesia)

LEE IS LAUGHING, but with deep understandable pride. Sometimes it seems that the famous flagship national carrier wins almost as many international awards as the nation's math and science students. But Singapore Airlines didn't just happen to become one of the world's best airlines. It takes hard work and a commitment to excellence—and maybe an LKY breathing down your neck to make sure you don't screw up.

Some years ago, the airline pilots threatened to strike for higher wages. Management wouldn't back down. A strike would have blemished Singapore's controversial image for order over law. There was no strike. LKY brought the two warring sides into his office separately for a long intense chat. Singapore Airlines still hasn't suffered a strike.

Strongmen have their uses, weak leaders have their excuses. Virtually without ideology, LKY admires people who get results. He admires foreign leaders who got things done for their country under the most quarrelsome of parliamentary democracies as well as takeover generals who got things done for their people despite the cavils of narrow-vision Western human rights groups. He favors no one form of government except the one that works.

He automatically opposes only one form of government not out of ideology, but out of disbelief of it ever working effectively— Communism.

His repulsion to Communism comes more from their severe Leninist methods than their Marxist ideals. He can tolerate ideology if it provides positive results; a regime that's a military junta is not necessarily to be condemned if its people are benefiting.

His quarrel with Myanmar's [Burma's] generals, for instance, is not that they are strongmen but that they are such 'stupid' strongmen, as he put it in an interview with me and Professor Jeffrey Cole of the University of Southern California in 2007. They so badly mismanage the resource-rich Myanmar economy that you can almost feel Lee wanting to get his hands on it to show the stupid idiots in military dress-up how to do it. They could remind him of another incompetent general who shouldn't be running so much as a corner grocery store, Muammar al-Gaddafi of Libya, a country with more oil than Mobil and a small population. The place is still mostly dirt poor.

I stare across at the famous man with the hair once so black and eyes that still are. Over his 31 years as prime minister (and then two decades after that in putative backseat positions), those eyes have seen so much that is both good and bad in man, and good and bad in himself.

In his general neighborhood, for decades the strongest of the strongmen had been Indonesia's General Suharto. On January 27, 2008, on a typically hot and humid day in Jakarta, the 86-year-old strongman died. His body had barely gotten cold when the Western media began revving up the recycled clichés about the cruel and corrupt dictator.

The accounts almost forgot to mention that the three-decade rule of this Javanese military man was remarkable not just for human rights controversies, but for determined and stoic nation-building. Thrown together more out of criminal negligence than geopolitical logic by the Dutch, who vanished as if in the middle of the night so eager were they to leave, Indonesia was a coherent nation only in the thrown-together, claptrap manner of, say, the former Yugoslavia.

What did strongman Lee think of strongman Suharto?

So I ask: "I remember when Suharto died, almost everyone said, thank goodness, the good dear old fogy's dead and the family is corrupt and good riddance and goodbye, and you stood up and said, hey, wait a minute. And you had good things to say about him and I thought this was very much you. You could have just said nothing, but you stood up and said your piece."

Lee fiddles again with his heat pad; he just can't seem to get it the way he wants it: "Well, because you've got to judge a man from where he stood in his society and where he had come from and what his ambitions were. He was a farmer's child who had joined the Japanese territorial force as a private and became a corporal or something. Then during the fight for independence, he emerged as a leader of one of the forces fighting the returning Dutch and he became part of the army. Now, he never had any secondary education, and his view of himself and of Indonesia was that he was the biggest sultan of all sultans and that was his view of his position, and as the biggest sultan of all sultans, he's entitled to give his family and friends the patronage that they needed."

'Sultan'—just when you think it's an ancient term consigned to history's dustbin or some animated Disney film—it gets resurrected to explain the contours of a traditional political culture in a way everyone can understand.

He goes on: "But in spite of all that, in spite of the graft and the inefficient administration he inherited from the Dutch who never built it up, he had to sort of improvise as he went along, and each minister sort of built up his own little administration or empire, but he made progress. It was patchy, it was mainly in Java and some cities like Medan or Makassar or Bali, but out of the chaos and hyperinflation of Sukarno [his communist predecessor], he brought the place down to earth."

I point out: "And he stopped the communists from taking over. In your view, that's a big deal."

Lee vigorously agreeing: "Or it would have gone the other way and there would have been a lot of trouble for this entire region. They were going to carve up this archipelago of perhaps 17,000 islands between China and Sukarno. That was part of the deal, but in the end, the Chinese could not intervene; they did not have the capacity to help, compared to what the Americans did for Suharto. So, he triumphed."

Survival. When your fate is to live on a small island of four-plus million, in the shadow of a sometimes unstable goliath of 17,000 islands holding 241 million people, you tend to get your facts down and your history straight. So LKY will not bother to quarrel with you if you insist on calling attention to the human rights abuses during the three decades of Suharto. He would just ask you to imagine what Indonesia's human rights record would have been like with, say, Kim Jong-il of North Korea in charge.

In Lee's eyes, America was smart to stand by Suharto. It was a lesser evil than letting Indonesia go to the wicked embrace of the communists. And, as mentioned before, he believes U.S. intervention in Vietnam, which we Americans almost universally bewail, gave Southeast Asia valuable time to catch its breath and get its anti-communist political act together.

Lee believes America does some very good things, then, inexplicably, forgets it has done them, and then—worse yet—sometimes positively uproots them! So sometimes it's hard to tell whether the senior statesman is more amused than irritated by American diplomatic incompetence.

He looks back to 1997, to the Clinton administration: "I strongly believe that [former U.S. Secretary of State] Madeleine Albright and [former Clinton Deputy Treasury Secretary] Larry Summers knew nothing about the history of Indonesia and were wrong in wanting to use the [Asian financial crisis of 1997] crisis to oust Suharto."

Lee recounts how the International Monetary Fund, backed by the U.S. Treasury, forced on General Suharto onerous fiscal-tightening conditions—in return for IMF aid—that could only hasten the collapse of the general's rule. He also vividly recounts Summers' blustery performance that at one point triggered a gigantic food panic in Jakarta.

"So, I told my prime minister, Goh Chok Tong, you'd better ring up Bill Clinton and say, look, this careless remark has led to a very panicky situation in Indonesia; better send somebody out to reassure the public that it's not as bad as it is. So, they sent [IMF head Michel] Camdessus and Larry Summers, and before they went there, Larry Summers came here to Singapore because we had alerted them; he knows nothing about Indonesia."

I jump in: "It doesn't stop them; just because we don't know what we're talking about, it doesn't stop America from telling people what to do."

He again shakes his head sadly: "That's right. So, Summers was here for one night. I spoke to him for about two and a half hours, together with Goh Chok Tong, and finally, he said, we must have discontinuity [in government—that is, Suharto must go now]! I said, you must be bonkers; you want discontinuity? What you need now is continuity! Suharto is just an old man running his last few laps, getting to put a good deputy in charge, a vice-president, who will take over and slowly unwind all these knots that he has created.

"But Summers did not think so. So, he went there and they imposed terms and Suharto decided to ignore the terms, and then the Western bankers and the fund managers pulled their money out and that debacle led to a collapsed economy. They are unscrambling Indonesia now for ten years."

He continues, with some heat: "And now the U.S. says Indonesia is the third greatest democracy in the world. So, they are all puffed up and the terrorists hit back and then everyone is back down on the earth. If you are the third largest democracy like Indonesia, why can't you collect these terrorists and stop them from propagating more young terrorists with the *madrasas*?"

He laughs and shakes his head: "So, Suharto had his heart attack, as usual, as everyone expected. He was old and his wife had died, and he was a bit downcast because he's got nobody to talk to and confide in. He would have gone down, as he did [without the U.S. pushing], and the vice-president would have taken over, the system would have been gradually altered. As it was, the entire system collapsed under the U.S./IMF push. Successor Habibie made a mess of it. Then Gus Dur made a bigger mess. Megawati calmed it down. SBY [the initials for the current Indonesian president] has improved it slightly, but there's a long way to go."

That was quite a breathtaking recounting. And, oddly enough, Lee thinks of himself (and should be so thought) as pro-American.

I say: "Are we Americans basically hopeless?"

"No, these are mavericks in the American administration. When I deal with the people in power, even Bill Clinton in the end came around [after all the troubles with Michael Fay in 1994] and he launched the U.S.-Singapore free trade agreement which the Bush administration completed with the present president of the World Bank."

I add: "Clinton got better as president every year. By the end of the second term, he was doing a lot of good things, particularly in the international realm. Maybe we should get rid of that deal where you can only be president for two terms."

"That's for Americans to decide. I don't know Americans."

American democracy, in his view, is good because it has worked—not that it works because it is good. Look at it this way: Singapore has lower infant mortality rates and higher life expectancy; it spends 4 percent of its nation's wealth on health care, the United States 17 percent. Maybe, I suggest, Americans would be better off if their system were more Singaporean than American.

I break the silence: "Don't want to go into that, okay."

He says this: "Americans will not change their Constitution because other people want to have a crack at it. They believe a chap with three or four terms like Roosevelt would be uncontrollable."

Not to mention a chap like Jimmy Carter, whom Lee would presumably find unbearable.

I almost forgot to mention that while General Suharto was dying in hospital, few foreign dignitaries came to Indonesia to be at his bedside. The first one—and almost the only one—was Lee Kuan Yew, visiting two weeks before his colleague was to pass away. Lee explained afterwards that it's not a perfect world but that respect had to be paid. This seems very Confucian.

The Godfather (Parts 1 and 2)

LKY DOES NOT see how it is possible to rule very wisely if one does not rule very firmly. Strong leaders make hard decisions that stick. Weak leaders make bad situations worse by deciding poorly or not deciding at all. This is what the oft-quoted Niccolò Machiavelli was preaching in *The Prince*. At some length his fabled analysis went like this:

"A prince … ought not to mind the reproach of cruelty; because with a few examples he will be more merciful than those who, through too much mercy, allow disorders to arise, from which follow murders or robberies; for these are wont to injure the whole people, whilst those executions which originate with a prince offend the individual only…. Upon this a question arises: whether it be better to be loved than feared or feared than loved? It may be answered that one should wish to be both, but, because it is difficult to unite them in one person, it is much safer to be feared than loved, when, of the two, either must be dispensed with…. Nevertheless a prince ought to inspire fear in such a way that, if he does not win love, he avoids hatred; because he can endure very well being feared whilst he is not hated."

LKY knows (and has elsewhere in effect suggested) that Machiavelli was on to something. He has often worried about the risk of meaninglessness and ineffectiveness if as ruler no one feared him.

Cultures of course differ, but human nature across the board reflects obvious and enduring species characteristics. Except in rare cases, perhaps usually wartime, slavishly excessive popularity is too often a reflection of mediocre governance. Great governance sometimes takes difficult decisions. No one likes to suffer pain even in the public interest. What populace is actually going to insist that vehicles be taxed for rush-hour usage, even though the result would clearly be in the public interest? Like the rest of us, LKY likes to be liked, but not at the cost of what he believes would lead to mis-governance. This is why his Machiavellianism is so often misunderstood (and, indeed, why Machiavelli's own original Machiavellianism is invariably misunderstood). It is driven for maximum effect; there is nothing at all about it that is insincere. It is a strong and useful tool of proper governance, as part of a range of tools and priorities.

This leads us to look at Singapore's great rival in the Over-Achieving World Bantam Division: Hong Kong. They share many distinctions, including being mainly Chinese, very successful and well observed by China. I think of its first Chinese governor in the post British colonial era, a man named Tung Chee-hwa. He is one of the most gentlemanly of politicians.

I say to LKY: "Before coming here I had a chat with Tung

Chee-hwa, a very nice man, a jovial man. I like him very much. I think he's got a bad press in Hong Kong and a raw deal, but I think history will treat him well. Anyway, he said, what are you working on? I said, well, I think I will be doing this book on Minister Mentor LKY and he goes, oh, he's a great man."

LKY, true to form, does not smile. He always makes a point of seeming impervious to flattery. Maybe he even is. I know I'm not.

He says: "Let me tell you my relationship with him. Tung Chee-hwa, I knew as a son of a great shipping magnate in Hong Kong. So, when the son was about to become the chief executive, I was in Hong Kong. I said to him, you know, the most important thing you can do is to get your education right because the British left you—deliberately left your people—with Cantonese as your language, and a bit of English for the upper classes to be useful to them. If I were you, I would concentrate on Mandarin and English; English because you need to connect with the world."

Lee shakes his head sadly: "Whatever the reasons, under pressure, he decided to go for English, in all schools which have been taught in Cantonese, to Cantonese and English; and the result is English went down, Cantonese became more pronounced and now, they've got to learn Mandarin because their customers are from China. And it is from our experience we know that if you try to speak Cantonese all the time, and learn Mandarin at the same time, that's possible; to speak Cantonese and learn Mandarin and learn English, that's impossible for the average person. Well, for the elite who can go to America and immerse themselves four years, six years with a PhD, yes, of course."

"So you see that as a strategic problem?"

"It was a grave mistake, and now their principals are coming down here to study us, but how at this point to change?"

I have always rather liked Tung and so I put this good word in for him: "Well, he had a tough job. I mean, he's halfway between the bosses in Beijing and then his political activity in Hong Kong."

"No, his problem was he's too much of a gentleman. He's not a politician and he got pushed around, that is all."

What he means, of course, is that Tung was *only* a gentleman. I daresay Lee would not take it as a criticism if someone said he were only a bit of one. Overly nice gentlemen tend to get run over by the overly un-nice.

Maybe it's time we call it a day. We had agreed to two late afternoon sessions. Maybe the first one is about to come to its natural end. I am beginning to feel a bit fatigued. What about LKY, now just a few days short of 86? Not only haven't I fallen off an exercise bike in years, I am actually much younger.

Suddenly he turns to me. I am certain he has read my mind, and I am certain it is not the first time. He says: "How old are you now?"

I am actually caught off guard by the query. Why would he ask? "Well, I've retired from UCLA, but I haven't retired from life. I just got bored with it."

"No, but how old are you?"

Still surprised, I ask: "What do you think? How old did you think?"

"68?"

"Wow. I am devastated."

"Why?"

"I am 55!"

"It's your white hair."

"I dye it to look distinguished." (Laughter in room)

So we call it a day. Tomorrow I am going to try to get off the global geopolitical and get beneath the skin with some personal questions. I want more time with this outspoken, brilliant, egotistical, haughty and successful—i.e. fascinating—figure.

Interlude:
Last Tangos in Singapore

So MUCH OF our journalism is little more than a fast intrusion in-and-out of a subject's life—public or not. But in this book we go a little deeper and stay a little longer. I need to explain what I mean by this and offer some background. I am writing this to you in June 2015.

These conversations with Lee Kuan Yew took place in the summer of 2009 and represented my last extended interactions with him. But they were by no means the first, much less the only. Extended interviews took place in 1996, 2001, 2004 and 2007 but these were not included in the first and second editions.

Now, to some extent at least, they are being added into this third edition. They help explain a lot. For when on occasion I was in Singapore and he happened to be out of the country or was otherwise unavailable for an interview, I would try to grab quality time with some of his key people, as they might be available to me. These included Foreign Minister George Yeo, LKY School Dean Kishore Mahbubani, super-diplomat Tommy Koh, and Singapore Press Holdings former editor in chief Cheong Yip Seng; as well as Prime Minister Goh Tok Chong, whom I interviewed in 1999, and in 2007 Lee's son, Lee Hsien Loong, just before he was to replace

Goh as prime minister as part of the orchestrated succession at the top of the Singapore government.

They all knew LKY very well indeed, of course. Goh was a quietly gifted politician with an exterior that came across as warmer than his illustrious predecessor's. And the son, Hsien Loong, was the proverbial acorn that did not fall far from the tree, providing an expansive interview that covered a huge amount of substantive ground. Like LKY himself, his son was not much for beating around the bush.

This Singapore-DNA of directness was on the whole a pleasant change of pace for an American journalist. I had no objection to it, to say the least, and American journalists who had never interviewed Lee or anyone in the inner circle and still imagined that it would be a cold or robotic experience had no idea of who these men were.

The advantage of having had these pre-2009 experiences and conversations was a sense that I could make do with less time with Lee Kuan Yew than if I had come into the project more or less totally green. So by the time of the two-day 2009 talks for this book, the mind of LKY was no more a blank to me than to anyone else who knew him in more than in a passing way. He had his strong 'likes' and strong 'dislikes', and when you talked to him you were in no doubt that his own mind was rarely in doubt. His unmistakable outlook of preference and policy was not the only thing that marked his political personality, of course; he was not just some academic computer that spewed out policy algorithms.

He was very much a human of both fire and ice and a personal charisma that could charm, scare or leave you cold—depending on his mood or aim or happenstance.

Leaving descriptions or explanations of these traits out of any attempt to truly understand him as more than the sum of his policy positions was a fool's errand. You might well imagine (and not be far wrong) that he communicated with his cabinet and staff with the artistry of the sternest conductor of a symphony orchestra. (If he had been one with a baton, I do imagine him as the late and overwhelming Herbert von Karajan of the Berlin Symphony. Under that man, no member ever missed a beat or played off key or made a late entrance! And the music was very special, even if not everyone agreed with every interpretation.) Yes, he was a tyrant in a sense—who could reasonably deny that? But look at the results he got, and decide whether it was worth it.

So it was an overall sense of Lee, based on the background above, that formed the mental and psychological framework with which I entered the conversations for this book, and which permitted a measure of efficiency and clarity in the process of these conversations.

For example, I knew from our prior meetings that he would always emphasize the need to base future geopolitical assumptions not on any certainty of China replacing the U.S. as number one but rather on the likelihood of the U.S. and China as either adversaries or co-dependents having to sort out their own national priorities again and again with each other foremost in mind.

Because of our prior conversations, I knew he would warn Americans not to lose sight of the vital importance of Japan, whose steely resilience to adversities and powers of reinvention he admired. I knew he had a preference for the American presidency of George H.W. Bush to that of his son George W. Bush (but don't we all?). But, perhaps surprisingly, he tilted toward the administration of William J. Clinton over that of Barack Hussein Obama. Especially on the all-important China issue, he appreciated the sheer relentless non-ideological economic opportunism of the Rubin-Summers crowd to the more judgmental tentativeness of Obama. In his mind it was important to keep everything real, and the only important things in all life were the real ones.

He would fall into despair if you mentioned the Middle East, viewing it as one vast black hole threatening to suck in American foreign policy in total. Due to our loyalty to Israel (well-known) and our eternal self-confidence (also well-known but less justified), America would squander the opportunities of the 21st century in trying to settle the ancient claims of that eternally troubled far-off land always surfacing anew.

About America he would marvel but also chafe. Endlessly a student of the concept of a nation's culture whose definition he was constantly trying to define and refine, he believed China's huge and predominant Han demography would swallow up and integrate any and all new minorities, in a far more seamless way than American culture would be able to socially and politically process its Latinos. The consequences long-term, he felt strongly, were obvious and ominous. At the same time, paradoxically, he celebrated America's cultural openness which, in his analysis, was the American way of meritocracy, with the happy results evident in the U.S. system of higher education, which he predicted would remain pre-eminent as long as it remained fundamentally meritocratic.

In this context, he was extremely proud of the birth of the Lee Kuan Yew School of Public Policy, in 2004, and its brilliant evolution under founding Dean Kishore Mahbubani, the country's former UN ambassador and preeminent global thinker.

But beyond his ideas and opinions and even prejudices, it was the forcefulness of his expression and the concision of his presentation that always struck me as his defining trait. Like Kissinger who would not be Kissinger without that swampy modified Teutonic accent, LKY was not LKY without that modified Oxbridge twang that punched up sentences without unnecessary adjectives and sometimes without subjects. On the whole it was a devilish delight to the ear as well as to the mind, where phrases would stick years after you heard them.

And so to illustrate his punchy concision as well as elaborate on some of his views, I have put together a thread of his comments made during our conversations prior to the summer of 2009. Some of these have been published in my columns but very many were not.

His original comments are encased in careful transcripts, and where a date would seem appropriate for context, I have included it. My aim is for you to hear his strong voice and observe the strong-minded man behind that voice, whether or not you agree with the view espoused. Just remember—journalists who follow and quote politicians are conditioned like Pavlov's canine to expect vague generalities, not pointed specifics!

For example, in 2007, Professor Jeffrey Cole, founder and director of the University of Southern California's Center for the Digital Future, and I sat down with LKY for 90 minutes in his Istana office, which had been the consistent venue for the pre-2009 conversations. My colleague was thrilled to have been included as a very last minute request of mine that LKY, perhaps rather surprisingly, snappily okayed. (He must have been in a very good mood that day.) From this 2007 interview—and then from others—is a condensed thread of commentaries that were anything but mind numbing or remotely conventional and seemed worth including here before we move on to Day Two of the conversations.

Cole, who is quite astute, inquired of the then-titled Minister Mentor about the inexplicable behavior of the Burmese (Myanmar) generals whose hammering of monks in demonstrations had produced damning public videos that had gone internationally viral. Lee's answer reflected his seering intolerance not of authoritarian government but of sheer governing stupidity:

"And in Myanmar, these are rather dumb generals when it comes to the economy! How they can so mismanage the economy and reach this stage when the country has so many natural resources? … It's stupid. … The Chinese, they've tried, and, in fact, we have tried to talk them out of isolation. I tried through a general called Khin Nyunt. He's the most intelligent of the lot. I sold him the idea, or at least he bought the idea, that the way for them to go forward was to get out of uniform and do it like Suharto, form a party, Golkar, and then take over as a civilian party. But halfway through, Suharto fell. So, it ended up as the wrong advice, they backtracked. Then they chucked Kyin Nyunt out. Meanwhile, I had advised several of our hoteliers to set up hotels there. They have sunk in millions of dollars there and now their hotels are empty. But, you know, you've got really economically dumb people in charge. Why they believe they can keep their country cut off from the world like this indefinitely, I cannot understand. We will see how it is, but whatever it is, I do not believe that they can survive indefinitely."

His views on China and the U.S. would help me sort out my own thinking:

"No, I do not see a win-lose, zero sum game here. It was the U.S. that brought China into the World Trade Organization (WTO). It was George H.W. Bush that opened the door, invited China to start selling to America. That was carried on by President Clinton. Clinton finally, with his then-Treasury Secretary Rubin, got the Chinese into WTO. You have got two choices with China. Keep them out—but the U.S. must have done its calculations, because if you keep them out, then you have them as a spoiler. They're going to do reverse engineering, steal your patents and where is the profit in that? You can slow them down, there's no doubt about that. You slow down their transformation but at the same time you are not benefiting from that transformation. If you go back and remember the 1980s and early 90s, you needed that market to grow but you never factored in the speed at which they would grow. That's scary. Yes that's happened and I think they know that it's a difficult transformation for them. It's not easy. They have got enormous problems. [But] I cannot say what they will do. I go there once in a year, I spend one week. I get reports, I read it but I'm not a China-watcher. I have got many other things to watch—I'm a Singapore-watcher! My guess is they're going to move pragmatically one step at a time. ... I think the policy will be let's grow, let's have more equality in the country and keep the country as one. Let's have no trouble abroad, let's make quite sure that Taiwan doesn't do stupid things which will force the mainland to act.... Where could China go wrong? Impatience; wanting to make faster progress than circumstances allow; pushing it too hard; taking short cuts that could set them back.... And if they push too hard, they will stumble...."

Please note that this was said in 1996! A few years later he was to add:

"Their problem now is convincing the world that they're serious about a 'peaceful rise'. [But] these are thinking people. You're not dealing with ideologues."

It was always hard to get him to open up about Washington, for obvious reasons, but he would say he admired the overt pragmatism of the Clinton administration's second term, which featured an aggressive business and economic engagement marked more by unabashed opportunism than carefully calibrated policy.

"Did the Clinton administration get it right by emphasizing international trade? Oh, absolutely. Back in the 70s under Jimmy Carter, your external trade was 6 to 7 percent of total GNP; now it's more than double that.... Fortune 500 companies get 20 to 40 percent of their income from foreign business. [But] they had [Chinese Premier] Zhu Rongji to deal with and that made the difference. Zhu Rongji was the man who pushed the Chinese side. He was backed by [President] Jiang Zemin. He did the sums and decided that if China was going to catch up with the world, they had to open up and this will force a continual opening-up, joining WTO and having to abide by the rules—and now they're in."

He was always worried about the superpower stability of the U.S. He did not share my view—and that of others—that the 21st century would be an Asian century, in the sense that the 20th was the American century, or the 19th the European one. He preferred thinking of it as a Pacific Century in which the U.S. remained a balancing Pacific power. This is what he said in 2007:

"I think in the next ten years you have got to extricate yourself from these problems in the Middle East. It may take you five years to get it stabilized and then after that, you gradually have more time and energy to think about the other big problems in the world. This is sucking up too much of your resources. To solve this, you have got to tackle the two-state problem in Israel because as long as that's festering away, you're giving your enemies in the Muslim world an endless provocation from which they can get new recruits ... to blow themselves up and blow the world up. How you're going to do that, I don't know.... America is so involved ... with Israel and the Arabs as well as domestic issues that it has little time to step back and assess where the real big issues will be. ... You have got to settle this issue with the Jewish lobby. If you have this as a festering sore, you get Muslims entangled in hate campaigns. I'm not saying if you solve this, everything will be sweet and harmonious—but if you solve this you will remove a cancer in the [international] system. Then you can better tackle the other problems. You are alone in this [Middle East policy] because the Europeans are not with you. Nobody helps you, but everybody doesn't want to openly oppose you."

One thing he was certain about—reverting to a domestic-focused foreign policy without clear strategic goals would be an error:

"For the U.S., the biggest mistake is to go back to Hawaii from where you watch the rest of Asia. It's an obsolete option. America has created the East Asia of today. You created, re-industrialized Japan. You rebuilt Korea after the Korean War. Vietnam? That was a mistake because you could have drawn the line in Cambodia. You paid a heavy price, but you got peace and stability in the rest of Southeast Asia; otherwise, the communists would have overrun the region. Yes, Dean Rusk [the much-criticized U.S. secretary of state in the Kennedy administration] was right. The biggest error now would be to withdraw from Asia. Order in Asia has been sustained by the U.S. and the UN. Behind the UN was the capability of the U.S. to stop aggression. If that disappears, then we are in deep trouble. Yes, you get the Hobbesian state of nature. There has to be a balance in which aggression does not pay."

And Tokyo must be a part of the balancing act:

"To keep the region stable, the Americans needs to have a balance with the Japanese working in tandem with them. Without the Japanese, on your own, you can't balance China. You're too far away. You need a vigorous Japan to host you and carry out the economic side of the equation. That's a problem now. They will take some years to come back. [*He's speaking now in 2001*] I think they can. At the moment they are mired in difficulties. But the Japanese are capable of radical changes. When they meet the crisis, they realize they have to change. They will change. [*The following now, almost two decades ago, in 1996*] From the world and U.S. point of view, the greatest danger is if they rearm and have nuclear weapons.... The Japanese can peacefully expand their military capabilities without alarming their neighbors, as long as they are in partnership with the U.S. I don't think the Chinese would say so openly, but they know it would be the greater danger if America withdrew from Asia."

In 2004, at a time when the American public began to realize the horrible blunder of our invasion of Iraq, LKY evidenced no appetite to be quoted directly, though he openly worried that a premature pullout would only add fuel to the fire of the raging belief of the terrorists that they would win the long game. But as for the wan hope of the development democracy in Iraq, he was marvelously succinct: "It might take a hundred years to develop a democracy there…"

In one interview I got him to let out a very considerable chortle when I said I noticed that Singapore's armed forces are in pretty good shape and so when was he planning to invade neighboring Indonesia or Malaysia?

> "[*Laughing*] All we want is a quiet peaceful world. We have made something of our lives and we'll be quite happy to carry on like this and help them get along and do better. … We started this LKY School of Public Policy, giving them scholarships to prove to them it's done by good governance. It's not by robbing you. I think that's an investment worth making because [students from the region] will go back and they will tell their media chaps and their leaders and say, look this country works because it's working like this: first, it's honest; second, it's rational; third, it makes decisions and follows through on those decisions. The decisions are made after very careful consideration of all options and consequences…. Your ethos is so different, it's to make as much of the individual as possible…. Maybe we can indirectly influence the governance in the countries of our region."

I mentioned in one session that I was a hugely interested observer of Indonesia, perhaps because of spending so much time in Singapore trying to view things from its lens. LKY was a steady admirer of the late President Suharto, despite all his flaws and errors:

"He did not prepare his successor and the country paid for it…. We took 20 odd years, you know. We did not do it in one or two years … I could have gone on. No one could push me out, but what do I prove? That I am still vigorous, then what? Then one day, I will be slipping; the vitality isn't the same, then there's trouble. So the safest way was to hand over while I was still vigorous. I was around to help my successor avoid glitches in his early phase. Because I had been so long at the control, it's been customized for me. So for two years before Goh Chok Tong took over, I loosened my control. I said, you take over, change the configuration to suit you. After the first few years it's okay; I'm not saying they couldn't have done as well, but there were little touches here and there which came from 30 years of making mistakes, and I could say no, that's a mistake…. When the [Asian financial] crisis struck in 1997, I could sit back!"

This was said in 2001.

Anyway, this was the sense of Singapore's founding prime minister that I took with me into the Istana conversations in late July 2009. I had had plenty of policy input from him, and some more was needed. But somehow I had to get him to talk about himself more personally—about his late wife, then gravely ailing, and his children. And I hadn't yet raised those old human-rights questions that he had answered over and over and over again. Maybe I wouldn't ask them. Everyone knew what he would say. Why not ask him questions he hadn't been asked?

DAY TWO

The Next Afternoon
at the Istana

TOMORROW COMES QUICKLY and brings with it a dramatic change in the weather. Stunning sun is stroking into Singapore and rain-clouds are nowhere visible. But by the time we leave the hotel at 4:45 p.m., the outside temperature has lowered to maybe 88° F (31° C). Somehow that seems an almost humanitarian gesture by Mother Nature.

At the approach to the main-entrance gates, the guards react as if I am an old friend. One says: "So, you are back!" The other guard actually smiles—amazing, and a nice smile too. After speeded-up security formalities, we are waved through to Edinburgh Road.

At least I seem to have impressed the gate guards.

I am in the Istana waiting room again, second day in a row, the peace and quiet soothing me. I am a little tense simply because this is the second and final act of the extended conversation. Maybe I could rent out for a month or two Sri Temasek, the yummy guest quarters, during the down months?

I am not even disappointed when LKY is running late again. Mdm. YY, the hyper-energetic press secretary, emailed earlier in the day that they wouldn't be late this time, but now they are running 45 minutes late. The interview, in the same sectioned-off spot of the State Room, is not to start until 6 p.m. I'm okay with that. What's the rush? The delay gives me time to reconsider my interview strategy. Maybe I'm going too soft (David Frost was similarly worried halfway through his historic and memorable interviews with the late President Richard Nixon). But you push too hard at these phenomenally self-confident (and sometimes all-too-easily irritated) figures, and the interview blows up in your face, serving no one's interest. A frigid atmosphere is no incubator of hot revelation. Besides, LKY knows exactly what he's doing; in fact, he knows exactly what I'm doing.

There's a rustle outside the door, time to go. I'm pretty sure we're on the right track.

Trouble in Paradise

SESSION TWO OPENS with a sartorial surprise: there is a dress reversal! This time Lee is up-dressed while I am down-dressed—me informally in Beverly Hills street chic: jeans, dress shirt and casual loafers. Perhaps psyched for the little photo shoot that the press secretary has organized for the break halfway through, MM arrives in a smart-looking mandarin collar jacket, dress shirt and matching dress trousers. This, of course, is public-appearance outfit of the Serious Chinese Man.

He looks more comfortable in these up-market clothes than in yesterday's garage-sale outfit. In fact, he looks sharp … but not fit. He still seems to be wrestling with pain, and perhaps a bit with age, as well. I stare at the press secretary and his principal private secretary, also now seated, and wonder if he is having to take painkillers. You cannot help but have a physical empathy for the ultra-strong man as he glares at a pair of rehab staffers lurking over the door. He complains that the heat pads need to be replaced or stoked up again or whatever, as they are not doing the job. He seems pretty miserable.

Before starting down the conversation road, Mdm. YY reminds us all—but especially the boss—that at roughly the halfway point photos could be taken in the garden. He is okay with that.

It may have been only my paranoid imagination, but at the start the atmosphere seems uptight this afternoon. The press secretary, I imagine, is glaring at me from out of the side of her eye as if wanting to speed the process up and get it over with. I want it to last as long as possible and even go beyond the scheduled two hours.

There is tension.

LKY explains that the delay to our start is due to the visit of the vice-president of Indonesia (whom I later was to discover was having 'issues' with his president back home and was thus in Singapore seeking solace and tender loving care from Minister Mentor). In part because of its convenient location in Southeast Asia, and in part because lots of people look to the Sage of Singapore for counseling and perspective, his modest office is something of a drop-in geopolitical outpatient clinic for VIP politicos from all over, but especially the region.

MM sits down and sighs. I avoid looking over at Mdm. YY and decide to break the ice by laughing at myself, which is not hard to do, of course. I start by reminding him that yesterday he had asked about my age and my response was pretty shifty. He laughed at this opening from me. I told him I would never lie to him again.

I say: "You know, yesterday, out of nowhere, you asked about my age and you guessed it as 68 and that was unnervingly close. I'm younger than that, 65 [big deal, eh?], but I believe emotionally I'm about 27; but your joust reminded me that I have to lose weight. But the reason I raise this, though, is I thought you might be interested in one reason why I've gained so much weight. It's mainly due to medication I've been taking, and the medication is a low level of Prozac for the diagnosis I had a few years ago of anxiety depression. In America, as you know, we have a medicine for everything and so, since I had alleged anxiety depression, which could be called 'normal life', they prescribed the meds. They say it's a very low level of Prozac (about 20 mg daily), but it's still Prozac."

"You've had to take it constantly?"

"Yes, I took it constantly for the last four years and one side effect was that it has been almost impossible for me to lose weight because I am used to having the metabolism of a hummingbird. You know, I would eat almost anything and I would pretty much stay the same weight, but now, it's become the opposite; the drug has lowered my metabolism. I think it might have improved my writing, actually; it's just so easy to focus on one thing instead of my going in three directions at once. [A half year ago, I gave it up, completely.] ... But I was just thinking that yesterday, you were talking about how strongly you felt about illegal drugs and drug trafficking, and I was just thinking, in America, we have that problem, but the other problem in the U.S. is the *legal* drugs. You know, we're almost going in the direction of a society that is over-medicated. You don't have that in Singapore, do you?"

He is talking now between eruptions of the near incessant coughing; it seems he cannot get it to stop: "Well, increasingly, we've got the highly educated on the Internet and they think there's a cure for everything and they've got the money. So, they go see their doctor and say how about giving me this. Doctors sometimes say, no, it is not necessary and try to dissuade them. But I suppose every now and again, the doctor says, if you want to try, here you are."

"But I mean, another doctor said to me, but Tom, getting depressed is part of life. I mean, sometimes, you get depressed, but sometimes, you get up in the morning and you're not one hundred percent, right? I mean, sometimes you're depressed, right?"

"Yeah."

"What do you do when you're depressed? You take medicine? Have you ever taken drugs?" Some authors have made the claim of Lee's extensive prescription drug use, both sedatives and stimulants, particularly during the mid-60s when the tense and tentative federation with Malaysia began to crumble. Those two years between 1963, when Singapore was merged into Malaysia, until 1965, when it was in effect expelled, had to have been among the most stressful in LKY's life: more or less constant acrimony between Singapore and Kuala Lumpur, Malaysia's capital, a full-blown race riot in 1964, and forced separation a year later.

One thing was overwhelmingly clear and one was not: it was clear that Malaysia's leaders deeply distrusted Lee for his ambitions, overt or otherwise; and it was extremely unclear whether tiny Singapore had enough of a critical mass to survive as a separate, independent state. Had I awoken the morning after August 9, 1965, the date of Singapore's independence and overnight isolation, I would have probably sought solace in anti-anxiety medication myself.

However, over the decades no conclusive evidence one way or the other has surfaced, and in my back-and-forth with Lee's staff at the Istana, it was obvious there was no interest in following it up.

"No, I used to meditate. I started meditation about 1992 when my friend, who was speaker of Parliament, retired, and was dying of lung cancer. He didn't know why he was getting lung cancer; he was so angry because he's a non-smoker. Another doctor friend, a Buddhist, came along to help him soothe down, calm down, taught him to calm down with meditation. I'm not sure if he succeeded because he's highly strung.

"At that time, my son [the current PM of Singapore] had lymphoma; he was under chemotherapy. So I told him, why not teach my son how to meditate? So he did, and I said, why not you come along and teach me too? So he came along and spent some time teaching me. I tried to sit lotus-fashion, but you know, at my age ... 1992, I was nearly 70, my left hip gave way. So, he said, no, no, you can do it just sitting down. Just close your eyes..."

"Focusing on your breathing?"

"Yeah, focus on my breathing."

"Yeah, that's a good one. It works for me too, sometimes."

"So, after five, six times with him sitting next to me, just knowing that he's there and he says, breathe slowly, in out in out. You can have a mantra if you like, or you don't like. I found my breathing slows down and I think my heartbeat goes down and my blood pressure goes down. So, I use that as a kind of escape from stress."

I am happy with his candor; it seems to get me closer to the real person: "That's a very healthy way. I've been working on that. I've been using the breathing exercise as well."

He adds: "That's one way I reduce stress, but I read somewhere that, oh, I've read in many places, that Churchill would sink into this panic-depressive state and then he would become very imaginative and active and start writing well. It's a kind of, you know, the brain then crystallized in him ideas and thoughts which have been unformulated. So? I've not taken Prozac. My daughter gave my wife Prozac once, but she did not respond to it; she just stopped it."

"And she didn't try anything else?"

"No."

Lee, by all accounts (including and especially his), has been far closer to his wife Choo than to anyone. He claims—and others agree—that she was at least his intellectual equal. Imagine: he's been in power since the late 50s and still a formidable presence in Singapore and never even the slightest whiff of a Tiger Woods or Bill Clinton-like dalliance! Nothing. And even his worst critics concede that, financially, he is clean as a whistle. Do I hear the word 'unusual' here?

His wife had been recently moved, at this writing, to hospital from their modest townhouse where she had been very gravely ill and unresponsive for some time. Even so, when out of the country, he would Skype into the room to check in on her. I find this very moving.

For a second my instinct tells me to raise the relationship issue, but I stop. What is he going to say? I just cannot do the tacky tabloid-magazine drill on this issue. Let's keep this book dignified (and therefore unusual for modern journalism these days!).

So we move instead to writing styles, how his wife had helped him, and his related admiration of Henry Kissinger.

I say this: "Super-K is almost incapable of regenerating a sentence that's a cliché. I mean, he really has an original mind, and I have to say, I don't want to be overly complimentary, but one thing I like about your writing is how simple and direct it is. It comes across as not done by a speechwriter, but written by you and it's almost… I was talking to Kishore Mahbubani [Singapore's extremely able former UN ambassador who's now dean of the LKY School of Public Policy] about this the other day, talking about how you write, and I said yours is almost a halfway-there non-fiction Hemingway. You know, Hemingway wanted a prose style that was almost minimalist. You know what I'm saying? It was shorn of anything that wasn't necessary and I get that feeling when you write, you're trying to get to the essence of it and get rid of everything else."

I could have added that you often get this intensity of focus in an oral interview with him.

"Well, my purpose in writing my books is to get the average

'O' level graduates, which is Grade 10 graduates, to read it and understand it. So, my wife was my scrubber."

Yes, I knew this—so this tack is going to work after all.

He continues: "You know, I'm an orator, or at least I try to be. So, I have [oratorical] flourishes when I speak. You must have flourishes because then you capture people's attention and you expand on it; then you're able to go back and repeat it, but not in words. So, she tells me, look—and she's a draftsman; as a lawyer, she did all the drafting of agreements, contracts, conveyances and so on; so she uses words precisely—she says, why do you want to write it like this? The 'O' level boy will not understand this. Why not use a simple word instead of this polysyllable word? So, I said, okay, I agree with you and I think in the course of the two, three years that she corrected my drafts, after the first year, I began to write simple, clear, crisp, I mean, no convoluted, sentences."

"But also, you have something to say. Thus you don't have to hide it behind a smokescreen of language."

He nods.

I ask: "You know, referring to our Prozac discussion before, you wonder whether drugs are going to level one up, or are they going to squeeze out that 'Winston-Churchill' creativity that you talked about?"

"I think there is in every person a natural psychological or neurological cycle. Stress sometimes brings out great ideas from you."

Lee could have been alluding to the remark by the French poet

Rimbaud to the effect that madness can be a spur to creativity. I can relate to that: at the opposite spectrum of poetry is journalism, which offers its full share of madness.

Me saying: "In journalism, we call it [stress] the deadline. That is our stress, that's our [creative] stress period. I'll be stressed out the next months writing this little book and trying to get it to the publisher on time."

Lee, for his part, confirms what I'd thought about that tough stretch of years in the 60s: "My most stressful period was, one, working towards separation from Malaysia and knowing that I'm going to abandon, at that time, five or six million non-Malays who had trusted us and joined the movement, and it's not an easy thing to do because once we leave, the leadership is gone, the numbers, the demographic balance will be different and they [the Chinese we left behind] were captive. On the other hand, the Tunku [of Malaysia] told me, if you stay on [with us], there will be bloodshed [in the country]; I cannot stop it, I am too old and too weak [he told me]. Maybe he was too old, or maybe he was just wanting to get rid of me!"

"Maybe they thought you wanted to run the place eventually?"

"Well, they always thought that and I told them it's not possible for the next 20, 30 years."

"Because of the demographics? Maybe they thought you were some political genius and would figure out how to do it, you know, that you were going to get a lot of votes somehow."

Lee nodding, but not specifically dignifying that comment: "And after I have done it [agreed to pull Singapore out of Malaysia], depression sets in, you know. I'd let a lot of people down and the anxiety of how do I get this place going. I brought this about. So, I used to wake up in the middle of the night and make notes."

"Because you felt it was all on you?"

"Yes, of course. Some [of my late-night jottings] made no sense in the light of the morning, but some made sense. I pursued it, asked my secretary to chase this one out and in the end, we made it. That's all. I mean, it was the pressure of having to do it. I mean, if I had taken some sedative, oh, I just carry on, don't worry about it. I won't."

I laugh: "In some ways, maybe my short-term memory isn't that great as it used to be, but my long-term memory ... I seem to remember more stuff now as I am getting older."

"No, that is a normal course of aging and there is an explanation for it from the neurologist. My daughter is one of them. Your short-term memory is kept in a different part of the brain and as you grow old, that becomes less efficient, that part of the brain. But your long-term memory is embedded in a different part of the brain and that stays for years, almost forever until, of course, you

> My most stressful period was ... working towards separation from Malaysia and knowing that I'm going to abandon, at that time, five or six million non-Malays who had trusted us and joined the movement...

get dementia or Alzheimer's. So, what I do as I get older is to have a notebook. I take a note and I say, okay, these are the things I've got to do. Otherwise, I'll forget it."

"Yes, I find myself doing that too."

"So, now I keep a tape recorder in my pocket, a digital one, and I say, do this, do that. At the end of the day, what did I want to do? There it was."

A rehab aide whisks in and gives LKY a new heat pad for his leg.

"If I may ask, does that reduce the swelling?"

"No, it increases the blood flow and it helps the healing." He turns to his right toward the rehab assistant standing by the far door, and says something like, warm it up again, it's gone cold.

He wearily turns back to me: "It comforts you."

There's Something About Harry

YOUR LOYAL JOURNALIST, catching his intellectual breath, takes another moment or two to size up LKY. The conversation has started off merrily enough.

As he is re-wrapping the heat pad yet again, I remind myself to remind you that in the old days some close friends and colleagues used to call him 'Harry', reflecting, in part, his British fine-school education. Sources tell me that in recent years his wife Choo used to call him that.

I stick to Minister Mentor or Mr. Lee or Lee Kuan Yew. I am comfortable with that. I probably could get away with Kuan Yew. But Harry, I would not venture into.

Sometimes LKY has a look of someone who could bite your head off. But at other times he wears this slightly wary if not wane smile that makes him appear as threatening as a happy cat sunning itself in the garden window. When I first interviewed him years ago, he was about 70 or so, but looked like he might live forever; now I am not so sure. He may not prove immortal after all.

For a long time in America, not one establishment newspaper columnist ever offered a nice word about him. Not that many had ever actually visited Singapore, much less met or interviewed LKY.

His worst American newspaper critic a decade ago was William Safire. The oddest thing in his attacks in his *New York Times* column on 'Harry' Lee (as his Anglicized given name would have it) was that Bill was not only a great admirer of Richard Nixon, as was LKY, but for a good period of time served as the late president's ace speechwriter. Their politics were hardly dissimilar. Maybe Bill's attacks on Lee's social-policy harshness were driven by the need to distance himself from Watergate by taking it out on "The Little Hitler of Southeast Asia", which was one of the titles of a column in the *New York Times*.

So I ask: "And are there any particular people in the course of your life that have made you depressed, like Bill Safire?"

Lee stares at me, then laughs lightly: "No, no, no. They are gadflies. I mean, they are not going to affect my work, they are not going to affect Singapore, and marginally he will turn off a few who are anyway not friendly towards Singapore, say, there you are, it was a lousy place. So?"

"You mean, you didn't get at least irritated over being called 'The Little Hitler of Southeast Asia'?"

"The what?"

"The Little Hitler of Southeast Asia?"

"No, it's all silly talk. Why should I be irritated with that? You know, when a man is reduced to using abuse to make his point, he's lost the argument. That's the first thing I learned as a lawyer; never go down to a shouting match because then you've lost the argument."

"You know, when I started my column in the *Los Angeles Times* in 1995, I asked Bill to give me some advice and he said, the trick is, make sure to do a lot of reporting. He said that people are only interested in an opinion column to the extent that your opinion is informed and inspired by reporting, that you know something that's really important that they don't. So, after a while, noting his fierce antipathy to you, I asked him, Bill, how many times have you met LKY? And he said, well, I never have. I said, so how many times have you been to Singapore? He said, well, I never have. I said, but Bill, you've violated your own cardinal rule of good journalism."

LKY said nothing, gazed at me, waiting for the next question.

"But then a few years after that attack, you two actually met, right?"

"Yeah."

"How did that go?"

"I was in Davos, and he said, would you meet me? I said, yes, of course. He said, would you mind if we tape-recorded it? I say, no, not at all. So, we had this conversation and he put it on the Web and he published it. Well, it didn't do me harm."

"Right, didn't do you harm at all!"

"I held my ground, he kept on pushing his. It's alright, that's the way life is. I mean, I'm accustomed to hecklers and people who try to put you off-balance."

"But who has criticized you or criticized Singapore and, in your opinion, made the most interesting case that you felt you had to listen to?"

"A few Harvard professors, I can't remember."

I like that. How dismissive. Only Harvard professors would be cited, even as they were not significant to merit non-anonymity!

But I let it go. I went to Princeton and Amherst, not Harvard. I thought that was pretty good, no?

Me saying: "Safire was neither a Harvard professor nor a big-time cheerleader for human rights groups. So it's a little weird, I think. But as you say, he envisioned himself as a gadfly. Maybe it was all just fun for him. But take the most conventionally, widely-known criticism of Singapore's from the human rights crowd, that you have run a deeply repressive government, God knows I wouldn't want to be in your opposition! Do you think the best answer to them is the Asian Values answer (who you are) or is it the utilitarian answer (what we've accomplished)? Or is it some mixed fusion of the two?"

> I held my ground, he [William Safire] kept on pushing his. It's alright, that's the way life is. I mean, I'm accustomed to hecklers and people who try to put you off-balance.

"No, I think my answer to them is, we in Singapore have a different starting point. Your outlook on the world and my outlook on the world are different, and my aims and yours are different."

Not a sliver of evasiveness appears in his eyes, the answer comes back straight and unapologetic. All the hard-worked years notwithstanding, at the moment he is fresh and unabashed.

But at the same time, it seems as if his mind is clicking back through the decades like a reverse time machine. He looks back at baby Singapore as if he and it were still suffering from some residual post-traumatic stress syndrome.

Look at it from his perspective: he starts off as a child under the flag of the British whose rule is so deft it seems like its colonial tenure will last an eternity. (Few outsiders realize it was the English who handed down to Singapore the practice of caning to enforce social control.) And then one day you wake up and Japanese forces are sweeping south down the Malay Peninsula like a volcanic force. LKY is now 19, but one smart-as-hell teenager soaking it all in. His previous world order—an English one—has suddenly been upended by a Japanese one whose authoritarian manner is far less subtle than the former's. The Japanese don't bother with caning, that's for the English sissies. Step out of line and they hang you. The young LKY takes notes, careful mental notes that he will never forget.

One cannot help but be reminded of the comparable conditions at the time of the birth in 1588 of the massively influential English philosopher, Thomas Hobbes. He was born a preemie. His mother fell into premature labor as England cringed in fear of the invading Spanish armada that was massed offshore. The whole of England was seized with fright. Forever after, her son was famously forthright as a stern law and order man, social peace enforced by the biggest conceivable cop around. No halfway measures for him: subjects of the state had to accept their leader as a maximum ruler or (he famously predicted) chaos would follow as sure as dark night after the brightest day; and the average citizen would be enduring life as the average hunted animal seeking to avoid instant death. Life would be "nasty, brutish and short" in a warlike society of "every man against every man", unless everyone consented to empower the Big Cop on the Beat—Lt. Law-and-Order being labeled unforgettably by Hobbes as the "Leviathan".

If Thomas Hobbes were alive today, his name might just possibly be Lee Kuan Yew, especially if he were actually running a country. This hyper-articulate Chinese Singaporean who speaks with all the verve and precision of a brilliant Englishman is, as a starting point—but only as a starting point—Thomas Hobbes updated. It is precisely because of his fear of Hobbesian-kind of deterioration that the progressive state becomes the necessary antidote to chaos. No fear is any deeper than the fears of a man dipped into the deep end of fright at a young age.

But his fears today are, in his pragmatic, data-driven mind, real, not phantasmal. His modern Hobbesianism seeks to upend obstacles and enemies as if one step ahead of the deluge of disorder. He runs scared so as not to ever be scared. In his heart he believes a crisis is always lurking around the bend, or coming up from behind; you just have to be alert for it. It's almost as if he'd be dynamically dead in the water without some crisis to confront.

Nothing better illustrates the Hobbesian instinct in him than the problem of narcotics trafficking and consequent drug abuse. He is no paper-thin American politician campaigning for votes on a platform of being tough on crime. He is a Chinese gang-leader-intellectual who is out for blood. For him, mere execution of the truly bad guys is almost too civilized.

Consider the plain and obvious history in his ancestors' background. In the 19th century, the Europeans, especially the British, literally forced opium up the noses of the Chinese mainlanders. By and large China's authorities, when they were not corrupted by the Europeans, fought the narcotics invasion. But they lost.

That was called the Opium War. Few Americans have heard of it. European history textbooks tend not to dwell on it. But unpleasant history sticks in the back of LKY's mind like the recurrent tick, or cough he cannot seem to shake. On his watch, at least, Singapore

> ...we in Singapore have a different starting point. Your outlook on the world and my outlook on the world are different, and my aims and yours are different.

will suffer no such repetition of history. Big-time drug dealers will not be caned; they will be hung. Some of them he only wishes could be hung more than once—for public effect and retribution.

He could not care less that American human rights critics are appalled by this official policy. He believes they are not aware of how the British once pushed opium on China, and he has scant respect for how the Americans have massively mismanaged their own drug addiction problem.

He looks at me and smiles, solemnly: "I mean, here in Singapore, any man looking as if he has been taking drugs is taken to the police station, which extracts three samples of his urine. One he keeps, one the police keeps, one goes to the laboratory, and if he is found to be an addict, he can be *forced* into rehabilitation, if necessary, cold turkey. Right? Not in America, no, no, no, you're not allowed to do this. So, the result is you've got all kinds of problems which you cannot solve.

"So, instead of settling your drug problem in America, for example, you go to Panama and capture the president because allegedly he's a drug trafficker. [Lee allows himself a well-contained chuckle.] I can't go to Malaysia and capture the prime minister because he allows drug peddlers to be in Johor Baru [Malaysia's southernmost city on the Singapore border] and allows my drug addicts to go there, where they are used as mules and bring the drugs into Singapore. But we control it by controlling what is in the country. I mean…"

I decided to stir him up a little (sometimes my questions are actually dumb by design): "By reducing demand."

LKY admits to everyone that he was impressed (from a social-order standpoint) as well as appalled (from a humanitarian standpoint) when Japanese occupiers hung up Chinese shoplifters to die in a Singapore square during the wartime occupation. He feels I should understand, by now, how seminal certain experiences were for him: being held by his ears over a well, seeing the British administer the cane, waking up and seeing shoplifters hung in the town square. So he smiles politely to cover his momentary (and understandable) irritation:

"No. *Supply.* Here is what we say to them: suppliers, you are a menace to society, you are a menace to your family. You become a thief, you become a liar. You need drugs and we've just got to stop it, and if you are caught bringing drugs in beyond a certain limit and, obviously, you are a trafficker, we hang you. That is that. I mean, Amnesty International says we have the highest number of executions per thousand of population, but we have a cleaner society, more drug-free, and we are not interested in Amnesty. We are interested in whether what we are doing has the support of our people, and they do [support the policy]. I mean, if it goes against the grain of the people, the opposition would have said, look, this is a cruel, brutal society. But they don't."

Hey, LKY—hold on a second! Amnesty has its own obvious agenda and certainly couldn't care less about Singapore in and of itself. But, at the same time, silence is not the same thing as consent. People may not agree, but nonetheless fear to speak up.

But if Lee is deeply troubled by this possibility, he has given scant evidence of it. As long as he's sure in his own mind that he's doing the right thing, he will take consent however he can get it. Elections every four to five years that more or less routinely keep his People's Action Party in the driver's seat are enough for him.

With or without parliamentary elections—and Singapore does have them—he certainly wouldn't let lack of consent deter him from doing what he believes is the right thing, if he could help it. At the same time, he accepts that motivating people to move forward in the right direction is the leader's job. He is clear on that. In some way, shape or form—whatever the system, voting or no voting—a true leader takes people with him, and doesn't try to beat them back.

The fact of the matter is that Singapore's zero-tolerance policy for drug trafficking, consumption and manufacturing has considerable public support. Once an individual is identified as a drug user, he or she is subject to a hierarchy of increasingly punitive measures and longer periods of enforced detention if further drug use is detected. Corporal punishment in the form of caning is routinely administered and capital punishment is a mandatory sentence for certain offenses. Between 1991 and 2004, for example, Singapore executed 400 people; the majority were convicted of drug trafficking. If there had been a public outcry over this alleged barbarity, the government would have surely muffled it. But that wasn't necessary. Singapore has a low crime rate and an admirable public safety record. Sometimes facts speak for themselves, leaving the comments of LKY, not to mention unctuous concerned U.S. rights groups, superfluous.

> ...we are not interested in Amnesty [International]. We are interested in whether what we are doing has the support of our people...

Citizen Lee

As these conversations take place, Lee is turning 86 and though I am younger, both of us are faced with the reality that our lives are comprised of many more yesterdays than tomorrows.

The man is certainly not politically un-self-aware. In 1990, after 31 years as prime minister, he moved gracefully out of the prime minister's office to make way for a successor (Goh Chok Tong, who held the job for 14 years before giving way to Lee's son). Lee is proud of that, rightly so. Historical giants like Nehru of India and Mao of China stayed in power too long and gummed up the succession process and their country's prospects big time.

This was not to be the Singapore way, not Lee's way. But while sidelining himself, he has been anything but sidelined from power. He still attends cabinet meetings regularly. Surely he enjoys more influence over Singapore's direction than Carter, Clinton and the two Bushes over America's on their best days put together.

We talk about aging gracefully: "I loved your recent speech on aging, by the way. You said, keep on working and don't retire. I love it, one of your best speeches."

"No, once you stop working you are done for."

A small joke: "I have this joke-theory, Minister Mentor. It's about people who retire. Did you know that there's a high correlation between retirement and death? Also, that there is a high correlation between playing golf too much and death? Golf is a killer."

Somehow he laughed. LKY has of course been coughing on and off and working the heat pads regularly. He still seems uncomfortable but soldiers on; now, however, laughter overcomes the cough like a wave of defiance and his dark eyes seem reignited with life: "[Laughing] No, no, I do not believe in that. It is just that I have been doing this work [of governance] all my life. If I stopped it, the stimuli is gone, I'll just fade away."

It is explained to him that a certain Los Angeles-based journalist is often—too often—asked: "When are you going to stop writing your stupid columns?" And the response always is: "When stupid newspapers stop stupidly publishing them."

Lee laughs again.

I keep going; I am on a roll (for me): "As long as they publish, then I am going to write them. Why stop? But it's difficult not to miss a step or two as time goes by."

Lee nods, confiding that staying in close touch with the people of Singapore gets very hard with age: "As I told them in cabinet, as prime minister, I was physically active in going around meeting people. I don't have to ask for feedback on what the mood is. I go about on my own and I make decisions based on how I have read the vibes.

"Now, I seldom meet many people in the old way. I make half-a-dozen meetings a year when I go down to my constituency. I used to go to every new town to see how their successful children were setting up homes separate from their parents, what they were doing, how they decorate their homes, how they improve their lifestyles, what they have in the refrigerator, and so on. Now, I don't do as frequently.

"Occasionally, I visit my constituency. So, I said to my colleagues, look, I have lost touch with the ground and I get my info from reading, seeing videos, TV and mining their impressions. When Jean Monnet became old and could not travel around Europe, he stayed in close touch with people who did, and he would mine their information. That is what I am doing. But the info is second-hand. I used to go by my gut feeling. Now it is based on what I have read, seen and heard, but not directly experienced."

Time-out for an historical note: Monnet (1888–1979), as students of modern European history know, was the post-World War I prophet of European unity. A gigantically important statesman, the famous French economist, in both word and deed, campaigned for a sense of common purpose and mutual interest among the fractured and oft-warring states of Europe. His intellectual and political leadership helped pave the way for the Common Market in Europe and, by logical extension, today's European Union.

That LKY would invoke the master Monnet in this or any other context tells you where his head is. You may perhaps suggest it is in the clouds—fine. But on the other hand it sure isn't lollygagging about in the bottom of the prestige barrel. For the leader of a small country, Lee thinks big, and Singapore has been his oyster.

Me saying: "But don't you actually miss that, or do you say, oh, I had more than enough of that getting out and about, thank God, it's over."

"Yes, but I haven't got the physical energy to do what I did. My physio [physiotherapy] just now took two hours. Because of aging, you lose touch when you are unable to meet people face-to-face. I had a better 'feel' of people when I was active and meeting people across all levels of society."

I say: "I know. One time I interviewed you, this was in 2005, and I think you were just turning 80, and the first thing I said to you was how were you feeling and you said, I am feeling good, but Tom, when you turn 80, that's a tough number."

Lee remembers and nods vigorously: "That's right, now I am almost 86. So, what is my purpose now in life? To use my experience and my international network to widen Singapore's space. I have friends who are leaders in America, Europe, Japan, China and India who date back to the 1960s."

It's the old saying: live long enough and eventually you get to know just about everybody. That accumulated knowledge and experience makes Lee into something of an international resource. An aging man can become hopelessly useless and debilitated with too much aging. Aging can render a once-fine wine sour, making it fit for nothing but the cask of condemned anonymity. But not this Chinese gentleman, not at least yet. For LKY, hobnobbing with the world's political and economic elite is not just a personal ego trip, though it is that, too. He is a roving resource of well-considered ideas and perspectives, a Chinese Master, valuable to us even when he is wrong, which he can be, as can we all.

When he met for 45 minutes last fall with Barack Hussein Obama prior to the latter's first trip to the Chinese mainland as president of the United States, it wasn't just a courtesy call. The American president wanted to know the thoughts of the Singapore legend concerning China.

> ...I am almost 86. So, what is my purpose now in life? To use my experience and my international network to widen Singapore's space.

In that regard, Obama was following in the tradition of his predecessors, going back to Richard M. Nixon. And, knowing Lee's ways, the young Obama received an earful. On the question and riddle of China, few world leaders have had more to say ... and indeed, have said it!

Some critics think LKY has too many opinions and shares them wantonly without even being asked. I don't know about this. Perhaps father doesn't always know best; but this is one father figure who knows a lot. They say in America that those who do, do; and those who can't, teach. But he does both. He has the country to prove it.

Fathers and Sons

LEE STILL JET-SETS all over the globe, making speeches and accepting awards and generally giving Singapore an image of cosmopolitan polish. Interestingly, the questions he is asked to answer rarely relate to domestic issues but world concerns instead, especially China. So he scarcely needs to live his life through the eyes and ears of his son, Hsien Loong, the current prime minister. He has his own life.

I am not sure how to raise the issue of the perceived nepotism. I know this is a delicate matter. What's more, as an American, I have to reflect that family is a powerful force in all politics, including ours. Our Rockefellers did quite well in elected politics. The presidency of the very qualified George H.W. Bush, who had only one term, gave birth to the presidency of the much less qualified George W. Bush Jr. It might not be too much of an exaggeration to suggest that compared to the latter, the current prime minister of Singapore can seem like Albert Einstein.

I plunge on anyway: "Well, it's inevitably a tricky business. When John Kennedy was president, as you know, he appointed his brother, Bobby, to be attorney general, and at the first press conference after the appointment, reporters raised the question of whether the young Bobby wasn't rather inexperienced to be head of the Justice Department. But Jack [his oft-used nickname] Kennedy deflected the issue, fencing off serious criticism with his great sense of humor, replying, well, I just thought I would give my brother Bobby a little legal experience before he goes into private practice. But now, you know, hey, your son is prime minister of Singapore. Don't people sometimes say, ah hah, there you go again, Chinese shogun system.'"

Once again, your interviewer is making a weak joke. The shogun concept is Japan-specific, of course, but we are playing with the idea of a Chinese-style family succession ritual.

Very quickly I feel, coming at me like little waves, different emotions inside Lee even as the coughing continues. Maybe anger, defensiveness, but most of all, pride—powerful pride for his son.

Immensely proud, obviously, but then a little defensively, perhaps: "But I kept him out [of the job when Goh Chok Tong was PM] for 14 years and he was on display for 20-plus years. So, everybody has a chance, including the MPs in parliament, to judge him for what he is. Every minister knows that whatever he does, whatever they do, he improves on it, in the presentation, queries and points when he was not prime minister. I mean, he has a very comprehensive mind. Have you met him?"

"Yes."

"How many times?"

"Three, I think, two or three."

"Where?"

"Here. I've interviewed him two or three times. No, twice. Once before he was prime minister and then after he's prime minister, and Goh Chok Tong once." I decide not to mention a column a few years ago—published, among other places, in Singapore's *Straits Times*—that coined a phrase to describe PM Jr: 'Prime Minister Google.' You punch in any question, and in a matter of nanoseconds out pops the relevant facts and figures.

Lee has forgotten this and mulls over whether to insist that I take an extension course about his son, then lets the matter drop, saying: "My wife once asked me about something. My granddaughter was there. I said, I don't know the answer. She said my father [now the PM] will know, and he does."

He pauses to see if the story has an effect on me.

He continues: "I had a friend in LA, who was a real estate man. He is a Harvard graduate in English literature and went to Cambridge in England to do a DPhil or BPhil, and he ran a university paper called *Grant* or something."

"*Granta*, I know *Granta*. Terrific magazine, actually."

"So, we became friends. When I did an official tour of the U.S. in 1967 October, I asked to see him. He had moved to LA and I saw him. Then my son did a tour—he did a spell in Fort Worth, he was in artillery—and my friend said, come stay with me, young man. So, my son stayed with him. He then wrote to me. He said, my God, this chap is really comprehensive, he is a mathematician, but his knowledge of English is superb. And this is an English scholar making the judgment. So, one day, my friend comes here and I gave him dinner and he put out a riddle, what word is it that means so and so, so and so, so and so. My wife Choo knows a lot of words, she couldn't think of it. I don't know as many words as my wife, so I didn't even try. My son came up with the right word. It just floored him. It was not his specialty. I mean, the capacity was, I don't know, what is the latest hard computer disk around? What can it hold? Whatever, he's got that kind of a hard disk [in his head]."

I say, honestly: "Well, I will tell you. If I had been founding prime minister of a country, which I haven't been and never would be, and then my son at some point took over and was doing well, I would be God damned proud."

He considers this: "Yeah, but at the same time, I must be very careful that he is not going to smudge the record."

"Well, what is the surveillance system there?"

"No, I think he is okay, he is measuring up to the job."

"But it is a tough time now for Singapore and for everybody else."

"Well, he has got a tough time, but he has got more resources than I had when I started."

Lee is referring to the relatively bare cupboard left him and his government when the British left. Now, despite the global economic downturn, Singapore may be the wealthiest country per citizen in Asia—and one of the wealthiest in the world. People here are thankful for their blessings, but sometimes wonder if they have the happiness formula right. It is almost as if they are thinking: Singapore is the little country that has a lot of everything, but is everything enough?

Fathers and Daughters

ONE CITIZEN WHO worries is none other than Lee's daughter, Dr. Lee Wei Ling, the well-respected neurologist. I have never met her, but I want to, especially after reading her statement below—anyone would.

Here is an excerpt of a year-end message she wrote in 2007 for staff at the National Neuroscience Institute of which she is director and which was subsequently published in *The Sunday Times* of Singapore in January 2009. She gave it this lead-in: "My house is shabby, but it is comfortable." It went on thusly:

"While I worry about the poorer Singaporeans who will be hit hard, perhaps this recession has come at an opportune time for many of us. It will give us an incentive to reconsider our priorities in life.

Decades of the good life have made us soft. The wealthy especially, but also the middle class in Singapore, have had it so good for so long, what they once considered luxuries, they now think of as necessities....

A mobile phone, for instance, is now a statement about who you are, not just a piece of equipment for communication. The same attitude influences the choice of attire and accessories. I still find it hard to believe that there are people carrying handbags that cost more than thrice the monthly income of a bus driver, and many more times that of the foreign worker laboring in the hot sun, risking his life to construct luxury condominiums he will never have a chance to live in. The media encourages and amplifies this ostentatious consumption....

My family is not poor, but we have been brought up to be frugal. My parents and I live in the same house that my paternal grandparents and their children moved into after World War II in 1945. It is a big house by today's standards, but it is simple—in fact, almost to the point of being shabby. Those who see it for the first time are astonished that Minister Mentor LKY's home is so humble. But it is a comfortable house, a home we have got used to. Though it does look shabby compared to the new mansions on our street, we are not bothered by the comparison.

Most of the world and much of Singapore will lament the economic downturn. We have been told to tighten our belts. There will undoubtedly be suffering, which we must try our best to ameliorate. But I personally think the hard times will hold a timely lesson for many Singaporeans, especially those born after 1970 who have never lived through difficult times. No matter how poor you are in Singapore, the authorities and social groups do

196 | TOM PLATE

try to ensure you have shelter and food. Nobody starves in Singapore....

Being wealthy is not a sin. It cannot be in a capitalist market economy. Enjoying the fruits of one's own labour is one's prerogative and I have no right to chastise those who choose to live luxuriously. But if one is blinded by materialism, there would be no end to wanting and hankering.

After the Ferrari, what next? An Aston Martin? After the Hermès Birkin handbag, what can one upgrade to? Neither an Aston Martin nor a Hermès Birkin can make us truly happy or contented. They are like dust, a fog obscuring the true meaning of life, and can be blown away in the twinkling of an eye.

When the end approaches and we look back on our lives, will we regret the latest mobile phone or luxury car that we did not acquire? Or would we prefer to die at peace with ourselves, knowing that we have lived lives filled with love, friendship and goodwill, that we have helped some of our fellow voyagers along the way and that we have tried our best to leave this world a slightly better place than how we found it?

We know which is the correct choice—and it is within our power to make that choice.... We should not follow the herd blindly."

I like the mature sensibility of these thoughts, don't you? Dr. Lee speaks well of, and with evident pride for, her father, but there is also a clear undertone of worry about the values-hegemony of materialism in Singapore that her father receives such proper credit for helping imbed. In her statement, another subtle point is made: that what we have in the present is not necessarily superior to what was had in the past, simply because it is contemporary.

So I ask: "Your daughter, the doctor, who is no slouch in the IQ department, as is widely known, wrote what I thought was a penetrating commentary in the context of, oh sure, Singapore has troubles and the growth rate is down and so on, but she wrote that it was time to stop judging everything so materialistically, raising the issue of Singapore's core values. Did that strike a chord with you at all?"

Reflecting a flicker of cold emotion, Lee looks off into space for a minute, then turns, and quickly—speaking in a more rapid cadence than before, almost as if a dismissive lecture—says: "I would say that that's only half-true, that if you are not making progress materially and you talk only the spiritual and the aesthetic side of life, arts, culture, you will fail because arts and culture is the result of a level of life that enables such people to develop those skills—leisurely skills, music, ballet, drawing, et cetera.

"So, you must have, you know, Maslow's hierarchy of needs; you must have your basic needs met before you can fulfill yourself, and the writers, the artists, I am not sure about writers, writers like Solzhenitsyn, the more the hardship, the greater his works.

I mean, he went back to the Soviet Union after the fight was over against the communists; he didn't write great works. Maybe he was older but…. But if you look at all the countries that produced art, literature, dance forms, art forms, they are all countries where they have reached a certain level of material comfort."

But that isn't her whole point.

There's no denying the need to have a good solid roof over your head before you try getting fancy about much else. The Lee Wei Ling critique cuts deeper: it goes to the heart—if there is one—of any culture that calibrates its sense of accomplishment almost entirely with economic indicators and measurable standards. Statistics can mislead. Heck, Europe could jump-start its gross domestic product number simply by abandoning its tradition of lengthy vacations and confining its holidays to a maximum of two weeks. But who in Europe wants to do that?

Just like my own home country, Singapore can give the impression of desiring little more, in sum, than more of what it already has got. Dr. Lee proposes (as do others, in Singapore and around the world) a calibration of the good meaningful life that takes in more than just the addition of a new car or a better roof or a grander home.

There is an urge to find deeper meaning in any country or culture that superficially would appear to have almost everything— and then is still asking itself: but is 'everything' enough?

It's interesting. A visitor to Singapore in 2007 would notice at the very top of the nonfiction bestseller list published by the authoritative *Straits Times* a book titled *The Monk Who Sold His Ferrari*. The title tells the story. One reviewer praised author Robin Sharma for capturing the persistent angst of the white-collar professional who wonders, among all her or his material acquisitions, if this is all there is to life. That seemed to parallel Dr. Lee's concern. (At the same time, to keep some perspective, the number three book on the nonfiction bestseller list that very same week was *Secrets of Self-Made Millionaires*.)

It is the fashion today for governments and others to assess a nation's place in the world by referring to common, competitive measurements: gross domestic product, per-capita income, et cetera. But life should be so easy to calibrate! It is not.

As much if not more than any public figure I have personally interviewed over the decades, LKY knows that money is far from everything. His unwavering appointment and promotion philosophy emphasizes intelligence and personal achievement over wealth and acquisition. For decades he has lived in the same relatively humble abode. Decades ago he spoke eloquently and creatively about the need for 'cultural ballast' to keep Singapore's souls from drifting off onto a dangerous sea of mass cultural anonymity.

To this end, he emphasized the inculcation of original language, especially Chinese, even as the populace acquired or improved its English, the international language of business. Not many national leaders think more deeply about the role of culture in the fate of a nation.

But I'm not sure Father was listening to daughter this time with all his intellectual might. Maybe not enough of us older folks are listening (as my own daughter, now 23, has said this sometimes of me). Too often, we are overly defensive whenever the younger generation says something. Of course, we elders can't help it. We want to have everything perfect for our children. It is the utopian instinct in us.

Dr. Lee's worry was about the damage inflicted on our humanity by materialistic herd-like behavior. It is a profound and also subtle point, and she is undoubtedly right. Singapore is the country that has (almost) everything. In its own way, so is America. But maybe 'everything' isn't really enough … or even everything.

Kuan Yew's Way

CHINA'S LEADERS ARE impressed by Singapore's sure-handed system of social control. Singapore, after all, is a solidly stable society, perhaps to a fault: Western critics regard Lee and his successors as little more refined than a gang of high-IQ control freaks, if not worse. But for the Chinese government in Beijing (and indeed many others in Asia, not all of whom wish to be on public record), Singapore's system of social control adds immense credibility to its policy recommendations to others. The Chinese place social order over everything else, a priority not too hard to understand with 1.3 billion people milling about; so do Western corporations and investors looking for safe harbors to dock and invest for the long term.

For much of Asia, what's more, the Singapore government gets high marks for aggressively engineering exceptional economic development without permitting options for messy disorder or, worse, bloody revolution. Ask Asians to vote for either the messy democracy of the Philippines, or for the comparatively non-competitive democracy of Singapore, and the latter's comfort, security and the other quality-of-life amenities would probably win—especially if it were a secret vote.

Many Asians were skeptical of the superficially idealistic Tiananmen Square uprising in 1989, for it could have led to a complete unraveling of China as a country. Almost everyone in the region knew that a China that came apart would be a tragic convulsion. From this perspective, the government's crackdown was a defensible option. Underlying all these Asian perspectives is a general political philosophy that Lee not only articulates better than anyone else alive in the region, but can brag that he has underlain economic and standard-of-living results that are the region's envy.

Here we ask him to weigh the relative impact of domestic policy and philosophy on international policy options.

I say: "Before I forget to ask you, when I was a young fellow, there was this philosopher, Frederick Hayek, who wrote a book called *The Road to Serfdom*, and it was a scathing critique of Communism and socialism and it was trounced by the American liberal establishment as being evil and wrong, but you think of it favorably."

"Yes, of course."

"Because he was right?"

"I believe Hayek was a very clear thinker and that he hit upon the eternal truth, explaining that the free market is necessary to get the economy right."

I think we are getting to something here that's beyond the anecdotal: "In that context, the great Thomas Hobbes, that 16th-century political realist and pessimist, overlaps with your thinking.

His recurring thought about the definition of liberty was that it was too expansive; that, in fact, it was so expansive that it allowed the citizen to slide into negligence about obligations to family and community and to state on the grounds of 'liberty'. A famous American screenwriter once put the issue of liberty or freedom this way: 'But take care, freedom is a drug, much like any other, and too much can be a bad thing.' Do you agree with that?"

LKY can handle being put on the spot, but his honest answer to this transcendent issue is one that irritates many in the West who otherwise would be more admiring of this man and his Singapore: "As I said, I am not bound by theories, but my upbringing in a three-generation family made me an unconscious Confucianist. It seeps into you, the Confucianist belief that society works best where every man aims to be a gentleman. The ideal is a *junzi*, a gentleman.

"What does that mean? That means he does not do evil, he tries to do good, he's loyal to his father and mother, faithful to his wife, brings up his children well, treats his friends properly and he's a good loyal citizen of his emperor. It's the Five Relationships, *Wu-Lun*. The underlying philosophy is that for a society to work well, you must have the interests of the mass of the people, that society takes priority over the interests of the individual. This is the primary difference to the American principle, the primary rights of the individual."

I say: "In that connection, the late and much-admired American neo-conservative Irving Kristol was also a modern-day

Hobbesian. His *New York Times* obituary read in part like this: 'In his opinion, his fellow GIs were inclined to loot, rape and murder, and only Army discipline held them in check. It was a perception about human nature at its worst that would stay with him.' This is very Hobbesian."

He nods: "The Confucianist believes society must take priority and if the individual has to lose, that cannot be helped. But Americans put the rights of the individual above that of society. You just cannot get some problems resolved."

I mention that Hobbes viewed human beings with more than a pinch of pessimism. He thought them at the bottom line so potentially vicious that they had to be restrained by state intervention from their worst instincts and actions.

LKY believes that the state needs to play a forceful and preeminent role in maintaining order.

> I am not bound by theories, but my upbringing in a three-generation family made me an unconscious Confucianist. It seeps into you, the Confucianist belief that society works best where every man aims to be a gentleman.

I look up from my notes and then at Lee: "One way of expressing individualism politically is one-man, one-vote. You say you are not a big fan of one-man, one-vote, and yet, the outcome of your policies in Singapore is highly utilitarian in a philosophically rigorous way—to satisfy the needs of the greatest number in the best possible manner."

He looks around the State Room and answers, staring straight at me: "Well, because unless you do that, you are going to have an underclass. In Singapore, that underclass used to be large numbers of Malays who do not do well in school especially in mathematics and science. But we've to give everybody a chance to make a living."

"But your basic point is that if you have one-man, one-vote and you have these lobbies and you have this deadlock of democracy, you are going to have that underclass, you are going to have the excessive freedom and it leads to drugs and everything else and, therefore, one-man, one-vote in a certain way is an impediment to a democratic result. Is that right?"

"Yes, I think so."

I think to myself (and no sense trying to compliment him, we now know that won't work): how many highly intelligent leaders in this world would have the guts to openly say this?

I tell LKY about a former UCLA student who graduated from the elite Woodrow Wilson School of Public and International Affairs at Princeton University and got a great job at a respected transportation-governmental agency in New York: "I said to her: 'I think I'm going to write a book on Lee. Now, don't get mad at me because I know he is considered a soft authoritarian, and you know I'm not selling out or anything like that. It's going to be an objective book, you know; it's not going to be a PR book or anything.' There was a pause, and then she looked at me and said: 'Sometimes I think we could use some more soft authoritarianism in the United States.' "

"Now she is 25. And I say, whatever do you mean? She says that when you see what happens to public policy and how it gets churned up by the special interests and the money interests, good public policy gets eviscerated."

Lee is puzzled: "Gets what?"

I cannot believe I have actually used a word unfamiliar to this profoundly articulate man. I explain: "You know, gets chopped up and diluted by the special interests and the lobbies in the process. You say to yourself, we could use an LKY here to set us straight. I mean, I think there are a lot of young Americans that are saying the process is not right."

Those black eyes seemed to shimmer a little: "You have carried individualism and the pressing of sectional interests to beyond the limits where the good of the majority is being eroded. Every time there is a shooting spree, the gun lobby works hard and the guns keep being sold. So, there is no end to this problem. One psychotic student causes tremendous carnage. It doesn't make sense. In England, they don't allow guns. But, now, they've got a thuggish generation using knives in and out of school. However, you cannot kill so many with a knife."

I happen to agree: "So that if you look at America right now, I think the system is not the answer for everyone; maybe it needs to be revised. So, the American ideology is we have done so well because of our system, but now it is occurring to young people that we are in trouble because of our system."

"No, any system needs to be revised from time to time. No

system lasts forever. Conditions change, some flaws in the system are carried to excess and you've got to revise them. You cannot say this is a general principle that's good for eternity."

"Right. In fact, Aristotle said words such as democracy and monarchy are not definitions of an ideal type but merely 'described different ways of deciding practical questions', and that is your view, right?"

"Yes."

"Winston Churchill once said, if you want to develop serious doubts about democracy, try to conduct a five-minute conversation on the issues with the average citizen."

Even the outspoken Lee didn't want to touch that one. But I seem to detect the trace of a smile. It's almost as though we came to the same recollection subconsciously. In a famous 1947 House of Commons debate, Winston Churchill was to remark: "No one pretends that democracy is perfect or all-wise. Indeed, it has been said that democracy is the worst form of government except all those other forms that have been tried from time to time." But after spending an afternoon or two with Lee Kuan Yew, you might be tempted to ask: are we now so sure?

The Confucianist believes society must take priority and if the individual has to lose, that cannot be helped. But Americans put the rights of the individual above that of society. You just cannot get some problems resolved.

By the way, I say to him, the most commonly used Western cliché to describe LKY is as a 'soft authoritarian'.

I ask: "Are you really so 'soft'? On the other hand, are you really such an 'authoritarian'? Are you content to be known this way to your people? If not, how?"

The answer comes back from the coughing LKY without irony or apology: " 'Authoritarian' means one has not got the consent of the people to your policies. My policies have been endorsed by the electorate every four to five years by a clear majority, never below 60 percent. I do not consider myself authoritarian."

> My policies have been endorsed by the electorate every four to five years by a clear majority, never below 60 percent. I do not consider myself authoritarian.

He would differentiate his view from that of the Russian political concept of a 'sovereign democracy' by pointing to results. You can postulate the need for strong state control and the elimination of true political pluralism in the name of development and stability, if you want. But then you have to deliver the goods. If you don't, all you've done is to seize power.

Time for
a Break

THE FIRST HOUR has gone well, but LKY is obviously still feeling it from the injury to his leg that requires physical therapy every day and the application of warm compresses practically every other minute.

It is time for a break.

We look at one another and agree. We get up together and walk out of the State Room. Immediately outside is a long cool corridor shaded from the sun; beyond that is a large sun-splashed plaza with a super view of the Singapore skyline. We walk down the corridor, chatting, then took to the plaza for a well-lit photo shoot.

The early evening is still thick with heat, but the sunlight is waning. About the same height as me, but thinner and much trimmer looking, dressed in the traditional dark Chinese Man's serious suit, LKY seems to revive almost spiritually in the equatorial sunburst. As the digital cameras begin clicking away, by pre-arrangement, for some casual snapshots for the book, we start joking, about everything, about nothing in particular, aimlessly—a stress relief from the riveting but intense Q and A.

The founder of modern Singapore is ordinarily a solemn, even stern man, with glaring eyes that with a whip of disapproval seemingly could chop a rubber tree down to size.

His lighter side is much less known, but it owns a sharpness of wit and mirth, and of course sports an intellect

212 | TOM PLATE

that drills deep into his character, which is sometimes self-deprecating, and bubbles up sometimes in ways that are often entertainingly blunt.

So I decide to play a silly card—a very silly card. The digital voice recorders are not around, so why not play a bit? I won't put all the banter back and forth in quotes because, unlike the rest of our conversations, it is not on the record, or recorded; but it is pleasant and even funny—and insightful, not only of LKY, but also about the United Nations.

Only half seriously, I say to him, you would have been selected as UN secretary-general a few years ago, if only you had announced candidacy.

In a light way I am testing the waters of his true ambitions. His achievement in leading the transformation of Singapore to internationally acclaimed success from the floor of a dilapidated former British colony and humiliated Japanese wartime outpost is the stuff of legend, to be sure. But the political canvas on which he painted is rather confining.

Singapore is not greatly more the territorial size and population of, roughly, the city of Los Angeles. In effect Lee could be put down as but perhaps one of the smartest 'mayors' in the 20th century. (Wise-cracking Asians from larger countries put down Singapore as that 'little red dot'.) That itself is something, but could he have run something gigantic like China? Or even Indonesia?

Or even the UN?

Standing next to me, LKY shakes his head and laughs almost hysterically at that one. He shakes his head again. The position of UN secretary-general is in its basic structure problematic, he points out, as if designed mainly for frustration and ineffectiveness. Taking such a post, though a distinct honor (et cetera, et cetera, et cetera), would prove little more than a personal ego trip mounted on the back of Singaporeans. The vanity fling would prove a pointless flirtation and obvious self-aggrandizement on the world stage.

And, he adds frankly, the job was not one for the likes of an LKY. Besides, he says the incumbent—former South Korean Foreign Minister Ban Ki-moon—is well qualified and is doing a good job under difficult circumstances.

We would surely agree that the position requires of its hapless occupant a polite and patient (and perhaps even reverent) respect for the UN's many fools, knaves, political poseurs, outright crooks and narrow-minded self-seekers?

Something like that, he laughs, with mirth cracking up a well-organized face otherwise reserved for rectitude, adding that—truth be told—he'd be an absolute disaster in the job.

Because you'd be too blunt, telling everyone off politically, right and left?

That's right, he responds with merry eye contact. That, he suggests, is the one part of the job he'd be good at!

214 | TOM PLATE

Then here's my idea, I respond: just take the job for a few months, during which time you will summon into your 38th floor Secretariat-building office each and every fool, knave, political poseur, outright crook and narrow-minded self-seeker; then sit them down, tell them off, watch their astonished reaction, and then ask them to leave and never darken your door again.

His crackling face suggests he likes the idea, rather very much indeed.

And after you go through everyone who is on your hit list, I suggest you announce your resignation and escape back to your beloved Singapore!

He says (chuckling), three months in that job, max, right?

Max!

I could do that (seriously laughing)!

You'd be very good at that, I said—in fact, exceptional.

If that's the deal—say exactly what's on my mind, three months, then out—maybe ... heck, sure. Why not?

We both had a good chuckle. We had constructed the perfect job, outside of Singapore, for Singapore's LKY, who's not that easy to cast in conventional roles. So we make the UN job into a bit of a joke, only a part of which was a gross exaggeration requiring a major leap of imagination.

The Singaporean Candidate

As we return to the interview table inside the cool and relatively dark interior of the State Room, Lee, rather suddenly, though quietly, asks to be excused for a few minutes, to visit "the loo", as he puts it, and to check up on a few hot incoming emails in his office down the corridor and around the bend.

Suddenly Mdm. YY suggests that the session end right now.

"You've had three hours," she says emphatically.

I am ungracious and unmoved. I am a pushy, vulgar American journalist, after all, and, oddly, somewhat proud of it. So I say something like, no way, I know you're trying to spare your boss from over-extending himself; he clearly is not only in considerable pain but running low on octane. But tenaciously I hold my ground, explaining that this interview is for history (how many more like this will he grant?) and I need every minute with him I can get. I argue that this effort is for a book, not a magazine or newspaper article. It needs everything LKY can give it.

Hers had been a worthy foray, and she took the abrupt but no-kidding push-back well. But I think she is not used to being pushed around by mere journalists. This is, after all, Singapore, not Los Angeles.

Sitting next to her and taking the oral battle in without making a sound is Chee Hong Tat, who has the actual title of Principal Private Secretary to Minister Mentor Lee. I am later to learn that he has an exquisite sense of humor. During the exchange with Mdm. YY, I think he was trying very hard to suppress a laugh while not appearing to side with either one of us.

Suddenly a somehow refreshed LKY comes back into the room after perhaps a 15-minute absence. His energy level seems higher now. I do wonder why. And, as if he'd somehow overheard the tussle between Mdm. YY and myself over ending this second session earlier than scheduled (was there a bug under the table that he could monitor from his office? Nah, I'm being silly), he looks at me and says not to worry, "We'll finish today."

"I've got only three or four more major topics."

"Go ahead."

"Well, how long are you giving?"

"We'll finish today." He says this emphatically.

I am happy, but puzzled. Did he take an upper or something? Nah, that's just the silly American headline-grasping journalist letting his tabloidian imagination go down-market.

But then, before I get going again, he says to me that he has something to tell me about the UN secretary-general job that's not a joke.

The background is this: by the middle of his second term as UN secretary-general, Kofi Annan was viewed by some of the big powers as a big-time nuisance—a showboating Third World blowhard. The Bush administration, for one, was looking for a successor who would be less flamboyant. So they began sounding out Singapore about the possible availability of Goh Chok Tong, who had stepped down in 2004 after 14 years as the successful prime minister and successor to Lee himself. At that point Goh, the quiet, hard-working, thoughtful economist, was far and away America's first choice for the position to replace Annan.

LKY goes on to explain: "So I am in Korea and South Korean foreign minister Ban Ki-moon knew that the Americans were supporting Goh Chok Tong for the job. So, when Goh retired, they wanted him to take this job on.

"Ban Ki-moon invited me to a lunch, gave me a swank lunch and said, is your colleague running for it? I said, no. He said, are you sure? I said, absolutely. He said, why? I said, it is not a job that he is fitted for. He's got to please irreconcilable masters, Americans, Chinese, Russians, never mind the British and the French. I mean, it is too much for him and he is not going to do it. What good does it do Singapore, whereas he can do much in Singapore and for Singapore.

"So, Ban came to Singapore to see Goh Chok Tong. And Goh Chok Tong confirmed that he is not running for the UN job. So, he knows that I am a straight talker."

"And then Ban announces and he runs. He gets the job."

"He gets the job because the Americans decided to back him, and the Chinese also backed him, and that was that."

"That is right. Do you think Ban will get a second term?" The likable former South Korean foreign minister was getting a lot of critical heat in New York as this interview is occurring.

"Ban Ki-moon? Possibly, because who else can the Americans back?"

"Yes, that is right, and who can Americans and Chinese agree on? Well, I don't know. I like him very much and have gotten to know him a little bit."

"No, he is, I would say, qualified for the job. He's been foreign minister of South Korea. He knows the frustration of working on problems that cannot be solved because you've got to try and make the effort and placate your constituency, in this case, the Security Council and the General Assembly, and he does that. And so, who can they find better? Can they find a Kofi Annan? Even if they could, the Americans will say, no."

At the time of the interview, Lee's views paralleled all that I had been able to find out about Ban and the UN and the roiling and often ugly international—and UN headquarters—politics behind that horrible job.

Rush Hour
(Singapore Style)

LEE IS VERY clear in his mind about the meaning of public policy. He defines it in the classic utilitarian sense: the greatest good for the greatest number. His orientation is toward results, not process. He is adamant about showing results.

His view on aggregate national wealth emphasizes its capacity for both undermining political stability as well as bolstering it. I ask whether increasing wealth is always a good thing.

"The bigger an aggregate wealth, the better for a country. Increased wealth and revenue can solve many economic, social and other problems."

But what about the growing gap between rich and poor, a worldwide phenomenon that's hit Singapore, too.

"If inequalities are too great, it will lead to discontent of the lower social groups."

Great inequality is feared not as a moral wrong but as entailing negative societal consequences.

He continues: "So, the Singapore government narrows the growing disparity as a result of globalization (high-end jobs being paid higher because they are in short supply), and low-end jobs, unskilled and semi-skilled, have been kept down because of competition from hundreds of millions of workers from China, India and the former communist countries of Eastern Europe and Russia."

This nugget of a thought is interesting: income inequality isn't wrong because all people have some birthright to equality of living standards. That is not his view at all. Inequality is a serious danger because it breeds discontent and the potential for dangerous instability. It is the consequences of the income gap rather than its mere existence that motivate correction. To be sure, the man with the Ferrari benefits from political stability as much as the man scratching out a living. The task of good governance is to reduce that inequality while not derailing the locomotives of economic growth.

This is pure pragmatism.

So you must fight, fiercely, any process or any doctrine that encumbers the velocity of progress. Good governance is the ally of progress. Optimal public policy is often both knowable and achievable, he believes, but the best methodology for discovering what is the best way forward is usually through a process of either comparative shopping (how others do it) and/or trial-and-error implementation at home.

Probably the riskiest way of trying to achieve the best of all possible worlds is through a simplistic or rigid democratic process that leaves blocking or at least mucking-up powers in the hands of narrow-interested lobbies, often in league with either demagogic politicians or backroom hacks. Lee will have no part of that. And perhaps nothing better illustrates the paradoxical paradigm of democracy-sabotaged optimal public policy than the classic case of 'congestion pricing'.

I chance a glance at the top aides at the table's other end, offer a friendly wink to his personal private secretary, who seems to be snoozing but who I know is as aware and awake as the control tower at Changi Airport, and wade into the dilemma of democracy this way: "You know, a whimsical comment that I make when I am giving talks in America and the issue of Singapore comes up is that I say the average public policy school usually starts with a curriculum and then they develop laboratories for administration of some of the ideas. But Singapore started with the implementation of ideas and then it organized a formal public policy school! I mean, in a certain way Singapore has been one big public policy laboratory— for real issues, in real time. As you say, for many problems, there is a solution, there is a public policy solution and it's your job to find that solution."

This time out, I was just being journalistic, I thought, but he tilts his head as if brushing off a compliment: "Yeah, and it is not that we are not going to be the first that face this problem or that problem. We are a society like other societies."

Learning from others as well as trying to teach them is always an honorable option for public-policy nerds: "Yeah, you Singaporeans are not Martians."

He nods, smiling: "So, let us find out who faces this problem, who has faced this problem, who has succeeded, who has failed and find out all the details, and then we come back and look at our case and say, now what is the difference in our case and then find a solution."

This is the full-blown Fox in Lee talking now, the Technocratic Leader of a Thousand Details.

At the Woodrow Wilson School of Public and International Affairs, the esteemed scene of my graduate work in policy studies, fellow students unanimously agreed that imagining an optimal public policy solution was always easier than envisioning actual implementation by the craven political sector. Politics and public policy were anything but synonymous. In Lee's mind, I believe, politics of the ordinary kind is an obstacle to extraordinary public policy.

I turn to Lee: "To me, the classic example, the one that always strikes me, is so-called congestion pricing. How do you deal with rush hour, which of course is the worst time in the world to be on the road if you are in a rush! But you solved the problem with congestion pricing. Well, why don't we do that in Los Angeles? Because you can't get it through, you cannot get it implemented."

"No, people will revolt."

"But until it is implemented, they won't be able to see that it's in their interest and that it works."

Lee clears his throat. It's odd because he's not a smoker and as far as I know isn't a drinker. Singapore, at least today, is not polluted. It seems as clear as desert air. Now he coughs, and it's a fit of coughing. I look over to the two aides but they've seen it before and act as if nothing is happening. I am almost ready to call in Emergency Service, seriously. Lee almost coughs the house down.

He finally stops, looks at me and breaks into a big smile: for people in Singapore not only have to pay a toll to travel downtown during rush hour, they have to fork over a huge licensing fee just to own a car.

"I knew that once people in Singapore could have a car, they'd never give it up. So, before it got out of control, I said you need a Certificate Of Entitlement [note: costs a bundle!] before a car is yours; and the permitted up-tick in number of cars depends on what the road capacity is. That was the first move. So, you bid for it. If you issue more entitlement certificates than is prudent, roads are jammed. Then a younger generation took over and says, well, why not have more cars and we charge them by the usage on the roads instead of just purchase? I told them, okay, okay, have a car, have more cars! But once you've got a car, you will never give it up."

I remind him that I hail from Los Angeles, where people say: "No bus for me!"

But here Lee admits he wishes he had resisted the younger generation of elite leaders with their lust for the individual and family car. But one man—even one with the colossal ego and determination and willpower of LKY—can only do so much in one lifetime. Too many cars, he knows, ruin a utopia. A true urban utopia would be a marvel of interlaced mass transit.

"I was moved on policy-thinking about transit by psychology. They are moved by maximizing road space. Okay, then you would antagonize more motorists. I would rather have less cars and get everybody to use the public transport, but a younger generation thinks this is the way to go and you [i.e., no longer me LKY] are in charge, then go for more cars."

"But at least you've got congestion pricing in."

"Oh, yes, of course."

"We don't have anything like that."

Under this sensible system, you pay a toll to drive downtown during rush hour. The economic incentive, therefore, is to avoid rush hour if you can.

Lee smiles. I really don't blame him. Maybe he could come to Los Angeles for a year or so and straighten some of our problems out?

Casino

AS WE GET OLDER, we worry about the young among us—
and whether, year-by-year, the age chasm becomes more and more
unbridgeable. This eats at you more than you care to admit, but
with LKY right across from me, coughing up a mini-monsoon, it's
not something that I really want to raise with him at this precise
moment. The subject is inherently awkward and, besides, I am
almost out of time. I am not looking at my watch or anything but
I can feel the onrush of the closure to these conversations that is
coming as surely as darkness will come.

And I am almost feeling guilty, as I know I am squeezing
every last second I can out of the afternoon, now rolling well into
evening. Few among our species are more relentlessly pitiless than
the journalist squeezing the last drop of life out of an interview.
So it goes…

Then the idea comes to me: Singapore's decision to enter
the global casino business. A pair of high-end hotel-casinos is to
open next year [2010]. But in the renowned fashion of Singapore's
policy-wonk-style-meets-denial (there is no prostitution, there is
no crime, etc. etc.), they are not called casinos but—ready for this?
—"integrated resorts". I take this term to mean that there is fun
stuff to do for the kids as well as the adults—or something like this.

I guess I have been to Vegas casinos once too often to think of a casino as remotely approaching Disneyland.

Me saying: "Wild and crazy Singapore, you're going to have casinos!"

He coughs lightly and nods, gently: "Yeah, because, you know, the younger set, the younger ministers say, look, we are out-of-date. So, one day, I thought, yes, we are getting out-of-date because when I was a student in Britain and I went to Europe, there was only place with a casino. It was Monaco. Now, casinos litter Britain."

"Well, that was quite a good verb: *litter*."

He replies with a positive eye flicker. "And in Berne, in Geneva. So, I told the Prime Minister, I have changed my mind. I think, go ahead because of the jet set and all the tourism that comes with it."

"Are you going to make sure that Singapore has the first truly honest casino in the history of the world?"

He pauses: "I am not sure whether any casino is honest or dishonest. We will make sure that the mafia and prostitution and money laundering does not take place."

That won't be easy but maybe Singapore can pull that miracle off.

Lee continuing: "The casino is inherently a fraud. You are bound to lose to the owner, right? I mean, you put five bucks on the dice, the dice has got six sides. When you win, they give you only minus 20 percent. So, you must lose."

I have been in enough Vegas, Caribbean and London casinos to agree with his basic point, even though the house takes out less from craps (I have been informed) than from any other game.

Me trying to contribute: "Right, even in blackjack, if you have a tremendous short-term memory talent and are a so-called card-counter, and you win, you are cheating because you win."

He nods agreeably: "And there you play this one-arm bandit. I mean, they've figured out a way. I mean, every now and again, there is a huge jackpot, but before the huge jackpot, they have collected two, three jackpots. So, I watched these people mesmerized, hypnotized, I am amazed that they are so stupid."

Somehow I decide not to mention how much of my youth was spent in casinos ... *stupidly*, I agree, is the word.

Lee explains his conversion: "But I said, look, our own people are going on cruise ships to gamble just outside of territorial waters, they are going to Macau, they are going to Las Vegas, they are going to Australia, well, so let's have two casinos here. But if any [Singapore citizen] becomes an addict, the family can say, bar him and we will, and if he wants to gamble, then he's got to go overseas."

I still sense a touch of denial ... family, no mafia, no money laundering, etc. etc. So I say: "Yeah, but I've got to tell, though: What happens in Vegas, stays in Vegas. I mean, a lot of middle-aged guys, you know, go to Vegas not just to gamble."

He sees the point: "I mean ... we will try and keep the place clean outside the casino; all the parasitical types will be cleaned up and we can do this. They know us. We've got severe laws to deal with those who oppose our system."

Maybe what happens in Vegas, doesn't happen in Singapore. I wouldn't be surprised.

"I mean, you take F1 [Formula One racing]. I was against F1. So, Malaysia had F1 and they built a special track for it and the young people say, do you know that there is a jet set which goes around the world? Fans and the banks bring their clients to F1. They say these are high-spending tourists. So, I said, okay, have one. So, they have one at night. Then the world saw a Singapore by night which shocked them because they didn't know that such a place existed."

"Beautiful by night."

"So, we move with the times."

Seems like a sensible gamble, when you carefully weigh the odds.

The End of the Affair

IT IS GETTING to be about that time. A soft-green pre-evening nightshade is beginning to color over Singapore. We both realize the end of this conversational marathon is at hand.

LKY starts to get up. "I am not a back-slapping type," he says, shaking his head, as I move toward him for a final question or two. "On the other hand, when I make friends, they are usually to be life-long friendships."

This is somehow moving—both awkward and elegant, simultaneously.

Sorry Amnesty and other critics. This guy is historic and important, and I don't know how long either one of us is going to live before "we go to Marx", as the old commie atheists joke about the hereafter, which they believe does not exist. But one has to take stands in life, and I am convinced Lee stands for something historically important. It may be something we miss when we put on our Western human-rights sunglasses.

He is more like some important nuanced nexus point where Plato (in his search for Utopia on earth) meets Machiavelli (who wants to teach Plato some real-life lessons about getting his programs implemented and his enemies neutralized ... and say to the great master: darn it Plato, don't be so naïve!).

Lee then confides in me, as recounted in the very first story of this book, that he expects an American journalist to achieve objectivity and credibility by lacing this account with non-flattering elements as well.

Neither a hatch-job journo nor a suck-up be, I always say.

I tell him I have three last questions, forgot to ask.

He nods his head, standing, saying go ahead.

God? Is there one in your life?

No, no, he replies, shaking his head: "I am an agnostic. I accept Darwinism." The great god of evolution, of course.

Then he smiles: "The religious right does not accept it. But nobody has come back from the hereafter to tell us which is right!"

That's a pretty good one, I think.

Then he lifts a tired but determined eyebrow. What are the other questions?

Why do you care so much about governance? I mean, you look at government as an art as well as a science, and you take it so very seriously.

"Yes. You are dealing with people's lives."

Yes, one is.

Final question. I mumble something to the effect that after you've "gone to Marx", will Singapore finally loosen up, as many have conjectured?

He pauses.

"It is for the present and future generation of leaders to modify and adjust the system as society and technology changes."

I smile. I've now spent more aggregative time with LKY than any Western journalist I know. In this rarified setting I think I can recognize a 'yes'. That was a 'yes'.

I lunge forward a little bit. I say the hell with it and I give this man whom everyone sizes up as a winter frost a semi-flamboyant hug.

To my surprise, he hugs somewhat back. It wasn't a backslap, mind you. And it sure as hell wasn't caning. It was, in fact, kind of touching.

I say: "All this talk about your growing older, I am growing older unfortunately."

"Everybody does."

There is a serious silence of some long seconds.

Modern Times

HE TURNS AND LEAVES. I make my goodbyes to his two hard-working and loyal aides and run into a security guard in the hallway. He is to whisk me out of Istana and into the hotel car.

This takes all of five minutes. Istana is either the biggest small government building I've been in, or the smallest big one.

But Istana is air-conditioned big-time, and so is the waiting car. Air-conditioning; it's everywhere in Singapore, thank you, Minister Mentor. One wonders what's next: outdoor air-conditioning? It is one of the first things the Masterful Mind himself decreed had to be added to government offices, many decades ago, when almost all of Southeast Asia was sweating from the perfervid emissions of the region's swamps, undulating deserts and Lawrence of Arabia sun.

Smart, very smart. Before long, government workers were staying late, especially if their homes weren't yet so outfitted. Working for the government became, well, the cool thing to do!

You slide gratefully into the back seat and feel the welcoming waft of refurbished air hit you like a wet towel of chipped ice. The car pulls out of the mansion archway and rolls down back

Edinburgh Road for the short ride back to the Shangri-la. I wave to the same two guards still at the entrance compound. They wave back. We're friends.

I allow a residual reserve of trapped, pre-used State Room air to escape my insides. The two afternoons with Lee are complete, on tape, in the book. This is done. It is all done. He gave of himself as good as he was able, I do honestly believe that.

But a part of me wishes it were not over.

This guy is the Clint Eastwood of Asia, a definite straight shooter. But now, how can I put it all together? How can it possibly be gathered all together?

There is only one way. One last time, we will return to the Isaiah Berlin theme of the great man/woman with many ideas for survival (The Fox), as contrasted to the great man/woman with one colossally smart idea or overriding linked set of ideas for survival (The Hedgehog).

Which one is he? Or is there yet a third category that Berlin missed: *Beyond the Fox or the Borderline Hedgehog*?

Here's where we can come down on this: Lee Kuan Yew's unswerving opposition to having any grand ideology or philosophy pinned on his forehead is on one level understandable, but on another, rather suspicious.

Regarding the former, consider this: that in the last century so many countless lives and souls have been ruined, and in many cases brought to a cruel end, because of blind obeisance to some One True Idea. LKY wants no part of being that kind of strong leader.

Rather, it is the dance of brilliant ideas that mesmerizes him, not some goofball, goose-step dance of the devil. Not remotely is he some crackpot Pol Pot, nor some hair-brained 'Little Hitler'.

But he is one Strong Man, that's also for sure. The most he'll let me and the late Berlin do to him—or, arguably, for him—is to allow us to stick the 'Fox' label on his forehead. That, you notice, he did give us. But he perhaps unwittingly gave us no more than that.

Yes, on one level, Lee is the original political street fighter, the Foxy survivalist, who, like the great Muhammad Ali, floats like a butterfly (words and speeches, invariably first rate) and stings like a bee (don't get on his Serious Bad List or he'll maneuver you into a corner, sue your brains out and you're done for).

This is the obvious part of the man; this is what you see at work. I give you Lee Kuan Yew, the Fox of all Foxes.

But on another level, that's just not enough, at least for me.

Look—too many ambitious, intellectually overarching speeches have been delivered, often triggering awe and often enough standing ovations. And—gosh!—consider that his own autobiography (two immense volumes) is almost as lengthy as Winston Churchill's. Think about that.

And how many mere tactical Foxes bathe comfortably in the pages of Plato, Toynbee, Huntington, et cetera?—the way many of the rest of us read the sports pages of the daily newspaper?

Solving the mystery of LKY is important not simply because Lee Kuan Yew may be the second coming of Thomas Hobbes

(Leviathan) meets St. Thomas More (Utopia)—though that's not a bad way of looking at him.

No, we must push on with our inquiry because his notable personality—brilliant, abrasive, tempestuous, successful, short-tempered, daring, even dangerous—may tell us something valuable about the nature of political man/woman, about the nature of political leadership, and about the nature of what we are going to need to survive the challenges ahead.

Pushing on further, deeper: supposing we liken Lee and his original People's Action Party team to an Asian version of America's own founding fathers. Their motive, in each instance, was to establish the best possible governmental structure and environment for their new country. But talk the democratic talk though they surely did, more or less sincerely (just don't ask too many questions about Jefferson's slaves, et cetera, et cetera), their credentials were elitist in the extreme: Washington, Jefferson, Madison, Franklin and Monroe (and et cetera, et cetera) were right-off-the-street commoners, right?

Sure, just like Nelson Mandela is just another run-of-the-mill Xhosa tribesman.

So what do America's founding fathers have in common with modern Singapore's founding father?

They are all elitists with a democratic cause: to improve the lot of as many of their people as possible.

So there has to be a big Hedghogian idea lurking inside Lee's head that he wants to keep private. There is, and it is this: sustained and sustainable progress is possible only when a gifted, empowered elite is in more or less complete control of policy. The complete corollary to that is his belief that politics that includes significant decision-making by the unqualified—or by the well-organized narrow interests, the lobbies—is the enemy of superior public policy. This leads to the third forbidden thought: that democracy, at its one-man, one-vote purest, is almost always the enemy of a practical, here-and-now, best-we-can-get utopia.

Please note: these thoughts are my extrapolations, not Lee's own words. Every word in this book that is directly attributable to him, he not only said, he also reviewed later on to make sure it was down exactly in the style he wanted. He took only a few things out, not wanting to embarrass Singapore. I had no problem with that.

But you and I have a right to take what a great leader says and use it to improve our own understanding and draw our own conclusions. Lee will, could and probably should deny what I have said above. I also will have no problem with that. He may even be right about himself.

But I doubt it.

Here's why. Lee's sole motive was never just power, never only political domination of his country. That would not have been enough; the Confucian in him would have known of his shortfall of character, for he is not an insincere human being.

His motive was to SHOW THE WORLD—and let me say it again, for emphasis: for all the world to see—that a Chinese leader and his Confucian people could in a united spirit do the governance job as well as anyone, better than most, and maybe, somehow, better than anybody!

Such an assertion would seem like quite a stretch to anyone examining the inferior level of governance in the world's largest Chinese country, right? That's the whole point; that's why, when giant China's maximum leader visited Southeast Asia in 1978, which Southeast Asian country had the most impressive set of achievements to show Chairman Deng? It sure wasn't mostly Malay Malaysia!

What's more, Lee and his elite and his people, reflecting Confucian acceptance of 'Father Knows Best', did not stop there; they decided to take it one phenomenal step further. Not having a Shanghai—not to mention an India or, indeed, a China—to have to govern (who, after all, was up to that impossible task?), they could imagine Singapore becoming a very model of contemporary governance at its best: using only the 'best practices', achieving maximum equity for all, constant striving for progress, all but electrocuting corruption (*period*), and maintaining the threat of Hobbesian law and order one inch below a cosmopolitan surface (all the while trying to give the impression that Singapore was just a Chinese Sydney).

So here was the post-modern Confucian Utopian dream: Singapore could indeed become like a (political) garden of Istana. You plant different varieties, give them proper observation and care, weed out the ones that just won't grow no matter how hard you try, and over time give birth to a glorious garden-variety of all kinds of public policy ideas and programs, from the celestial to the mundane (citizens are bilingual, congestion pricing, no gum sticking, we-cane-your-butt-if-you-get-out-of-line, everyone-gets-good-health-proper-education-home-ownership, et cetera, et cetera).

So how do we best describe or depict this Garden of Political Istana?

We all know that classic heavenly utopias do not really exist on this polluted planet. And some alleged utopias are nothing but flaw-ridden. The Soviet rendition of heaven-on-earth was most often a hell-on-earth. Fidel Castro may have had the best of intentions 50-plus years ago when his band of ideological communists swept down from the mountain and seized Cuba; but in due course their utopian ideology and Stalinist governance made everyone (except the party elite) more or less equally … poor. And whatever we might say of Mao Zedong and his Worker's Paradise perhaps, well, at this point, it is better left unsaid. Then there's Pol Pot's hellhole Cambodia … and on and on.

By contrast, Lee Kuan Yew walked the walk of utopian-inspired governance better than so many others. With enormous effort, he pieced together, layer by layer, a skilled governing elite (like a Plato, but advised by Machiavelli)—encompassing all the important professions, not just governmental—that pushed his country to the globe's top league of accomplished economies. And with remarkable self-awareness he sought to avoid the poison of purist political and economic ideology that undid otherwise great men like India's Nehru, without descending into the creepy cronyism and crippling corruption characteristic of so many other egomaniacal regimes around the world.

He, his inner elite and his people did all this while hewing in an almost intimate way to two political ideas. One was the vision of Plato, elevated to the scale of a nation-state, and the other was the hard-nosed methodology of Machiavelli.

It seems to me that Lee Kuan Yew is where Plato meets Machiavelli—in the special land of Confucius. But did it work? It mostly has, and is. Had he been nothing more remarkable than a Machiavellian thug, his country would have descended into mere cynicism and manipulation; just the former, and the whole ambitious neo-utopian project would never have gotten off the drawing board. But using (when available!) scientific methods of policy and governance, maneuvering into power a highly educated and motivated elite, and scaring the living hell out of anyone who stood in his way, including, potentially, a media that might get into trouble-making or agenda-setting, Lee Kuan Yew achieved pretty much what he set out to do.

Think about that: for all the hot air of politicians, for all the complex modeling and intellectual posturing of academics, for all the high-minded moral statements of the moralists and activists, Singapore took it all in, worked itself to the bone, and got a whole lot of it done.

Utopia of course comes from a Greek word and it can mean 'no place' or 'doesn't exist'. The adjective 'utopian' is often used to suggest implausibility, if not impossibility. The plural 'utopians' can be used to mean 'starry-eyed dreamers'. And surely one citizen's utopia is another citizen's hell.

Singapore is certainly no utopia for drug dealers or drug users; it's anything but heaven on earth for opponents of the governing party and government. Among other privileged acolytes you find preening in the West, criminal trial lawyers are given a much less rope in Lee's Singapore. First Amendment absolutists will find no utopian joy in the generally subtle but clearly limiting red lines placed around the news media.

So, one way or the other, we agree, earth has no utopia. Singapore resides on the planet earth. Therefore, Singapore is no perfect utopia.

So what is the next best thing? And what should we call it?

The thing itself may well be Singapore itself, faults and all. It is this era's Neo-Utopia, a living example of getting a place into as utopian a shape as is humanely possible.

That is Lee's achievement. Lee is a Pragmatic Confucian Neo-Utopian. That's the very big idea: Singapore as a very small place that became a very big deal.

Yes, it's not perfect. No *real-world* Utopia is. But maybe we need to start being more realistic about what we should expect from our neo-utopias, if we want to recognize them for what they have to offer. For what was done in Singapore, over a mere half dozen decades, had to have been the work of some kind of Hedgehog.

Absolutely.

Afterword

Judgment at Singapore

IT IS HARD TO BELIEVE.

It is now little more than three years after the Istana conversations, and Lee Kuan Yew is no longer in the cabinet of Singapore. The explosive national elections of 2011 seemed to cut the long-dominant People's Action Party down to size, even while it retained a lock on parliament. The voters' cautionary rebuff to the PAP heralded a new chapter. George Yeo, the brainy foreign minister, lost his seat, and both Minister Mentor Lee and Senior Minister Goh Chok Tong had to accept that this was the political end of their extraordinary run. By U.S. standards, the PAP's winning margin was a landslide. But by Singapore standards, it was almost abject rejection.

And while the tiny country was churning politically, it was trying to become hip. There were alluring casinos (mainly for tourists), a new vibrant arts scene, and a sense that a younger generation was pushing up from below to challenge the status quo. Massive and intense interactivity on the Internet (an intrinsically anti-authoritarian technology spawned in fact by official embrace years before) seemed to infuse debate with new openness. Singapore's hierarchies seemed a bit more horizontal than vertical.

And there was no doubt that modern Singapore's founder

was himself a changed man. While not quite a total recluse, the heretofore-nonstop Lee threw in his cards and kicked back. The death in 2010 of his beloved wife, Kwa Geok Choo, after a long illness, had already rocked him. And his departure from government had signaled the beginning of the final chapter.

Three years before that, in an Istana office interview, I asked him how he was feeling.

"Ageing rather fitfully as we all do, but when you're past 80, it's a pretty steep climb. I think if you retire, the idea of just reading books and playing golf ... you just disintegrate."

Me adding (as usual trying to lighten things up): "There's such a high correlation between people who retire and play golf, and die, right? If you don't play golf and don't retire ... follow the logic!"

He nodded with a wan smile: "You have to have something more than that. You have got to wake up every morning feeling there's something worth doing and you're not just lying back and coasting along. Once you coast along, it's finished."

He very well knew this.

Even so, now in 2013, rumor had it that some of Lee's afternoons would be spent reclusively, sometimes resting in a hotel's poolside cabana, overlooking downtown. To be sure, this proud man was still capable of delivering a speech, and was more than capable of huffily ambling out, under his own steel, on a debate in parliament whose substantive content he found wanting. But LKY was at ease now and knew his incredible run as Singapore's modern founder was well over.

246 | TOM PLATE

Alas, the Internet, which brought un-Singapore-like messiness to the political debate, seemed almost to be ghoulish about it. It was Tuesday, August 7, 2012, and the blogs and Twitter rumor mills were spewing out the spectacular spark that he had been admitted to hospital or even had died. Many did not buy that, of course, myself included, especially when my home fax machine was aroused around 3 a.m. the next day, August 8. It was from him.

I had asked for it. Though respecting his desire for the solace of his own company, and believing that we had rolled over many vast landscapes of issues and events in our conversations, I nonetheless wanted him to have the last say if he wished—the final conversation, as it were. I invited him to have one more go at it, if only via email.

His answer was true to the core of his being—blunt, final, sensible, and even off-hand witty. The fax, in his own handwriting, read simply: "Tom: Nothing new to add. LKY. 8 Aug 2012."

I had to laugh. He was right.

After all, what else was there to say? For more than five decades in high positions, speaking not just to his fellow citizens at home but offering wisdoms at international events everywhere, Lee had more than said his piece. And then some!

Sometimes, in truth, many Singaporeans felt he had said too much, and were relieved that he had stopped lecturing them on almost everything under the equatorial sun. He seemed to have in stock an answer for everything. From the ideal size of families to the proper supply of physicians for the nation, there seemed no end to what he had to say. And Singapore had to listen. It was as if he regarded limitations on his expertise as challenges to the authority of his governance. His outspoken views did not always play well internationally. His negative comments about the rapid growth of the Latino population in the U.S., expressed earlier in this book, might well be judged as prejudiced. My first interview with him, in 1996, ended with the thought that the reason Asian students tend to do better in math and science had something to do with the "slightly different balance in the Asian brain, more numerate than literate".

The journalist in me adores the outspokenness. But we are a craven breed. The human being in me recoils at the generalizations. But no matter. No more. It was all over. For now the time had come for history to begin to have its say.

Lee is a better listener than generally acknowledged. As you have just witnessed in this book, he's a person with whom one can have an actual conversation. In fact, if you are not readily intimidated, he is as easy to talk to as, say, Bill Clinton.

Communication of many kinds—verbal as well as symbolic—is required to govern well. Mass politics requires a leader's persuasion to maximize political effectiveness. He knew what he wanted for his Singapore, but a driven utilitarian, Lee judged himself, almost ideologically, by standards that could be scientifically measured.

He was almost always in a deliberate rush to achieve. Per-capita income. International competitiveness. Scholastic scores. Low inflation. High employment. He wanted nothing to stand in the way of measurable achievements. He hated unnecessary delays, such as from uninformed debate, which of course is the essence of mass democracy. But unless he were to do away with elections altogether, he had to know what his people thought, even if much of it seemed to him thoughtless—or in any event, uninformed. The leader always has to carry the people with him, as he'd say.

The ancient Greek thinkers understood the core problem. One perceptive modern-day interpreter was Michel Foucault, the late French philosopher who used to lecture about Greek thought at the College de France. He accepted their insights about the severe contradiction at the heart of the very concept of democracy.

And the Greeks had a word for that. Two words, actually.

The first was *parrhesia*, which sort of means 'truth-telling' or 'free, frank speech' in a profound way. The theoretical *sine qua non* of superior governance means the best decisions are produced by the best thought and information and discussion. Not everyone can do that. So ongoing tension exists between *parrhesia* and its opposite, *isegoria*. This latter means (sort of) 'everyone has an equal and absolute right to speak in public debate, whatever the truth value'. (This is to say: no matter how uninformed or, arguably, even stupid.)

The first speaks to Maximum Truth, political correctness notwithstanding, people's feelings notwithstanding; and said *parrhesia* speech must be pure and wise and, above all, anything but self-seeking.

The second speaks to accepting that everyone is speech-equal and every citizen needs to have her or his say and should be equally involved in the public debate, no matter how little they may know or however self-seeking they may be.

Everyone and anyone can do their *isegoria*. That's easy enough. But *parrhesia*—this is something else entirely. The two are in opposition: Truth-telling and speech-equality are anything but the same.

Foucault used to suggest that democracy could either affirm equality of public speech at the expense of *parrhesia* or affirm quality of public discourse at the expense of *isegoria*. My hypothesis is that LKY, who did not suffer fools or foolish comment readily, was a fervent admirer of *parrhesia* and not of *isegoria*. He thought the latter, if left unchecked by proper educated authority, would degrade Singapore's polity and handicap its rate of progress.

To extrapolate, Lee followed in the footsteps of Plato, who describes his mentor Socrates as sometimes distrusting the utility of truth-telling to the masses. Wrote Foucault by way of explanation: "The powerlessness of true discourse in democracy is not due, of course, to true discourse, that is, to the fact that discourse is true. It is due to the very structure of democracy."

Bring Lee back into this discussion.

Remember, he honestly admitted to us (with a plain-spoken directness I had not seen elsewhere before, and have not heard from him since) that the *ideology* of democracy left him cold. And

I have to tell you that, when he said it toward the end of our first day of conversations—with absolutely no apology whatsoever—the comment seemed to me breathtaking in its utter disregard of political correctness or polite qualification. Said Lee to us: "I do not believe that one-man, one-vote, in either the U.S. format or the British format or the French format, is the final position."

Public truth-telling and real-world politics makes for a very rough fit when trying to co-exist in a political system. This is not something political leaders say publicly. But the difference between the individual speaking the truth and wanting the truth to predominate, on the one hand, and the equal right of all to speak in comparable volume even if it runs the risk of advancing untruthfulness—this is tough one.

Lee of course was no Old Testament prophet but a modern Machiavellian political leader with a strategic vision—perhaps even of a Plato. As a utilitarian pragmatist who mainly wanted to get good things done properly and, if possible, rapidly, he was not a sainted ideologue about this, or about anything else. He knew what he could get away with and was a master of rhetorical nuance. He was often accused of controlling the courts but—whatever the truth of that—in fact, as a close associate put it to me, "everything he did or said had to be legally defensible". He could rouse a crowd with the best of them.

His goal was not to stay in power for its own sake and loot, as with some Third World despot, but to deploy that power to improve Singapore dramatically and impress on neighbors how it can be done. He was often in a rush. Failures slammed progress into reverse. So what he could not tolerate was ineffectiveness, especially cloaked in ideological purity. Ideological arguments were for professors of the academic and arcane.

"Singapore is not a 4,000-year culture," he told me in an interview in 2007. "This is an immigrant community that started in 1819. It's an immigrant community that left its moorings and therefore, knowing it's sailing to unchartered seas, is guided by the stars. I say let's follow the stars and they said okay, let's try. And we've succeeded and here we are, but has it really taken root? No. It's just worked for the time being. If it doesn't [continue to] work, again, we say let's try something else. This [Singapore's current way] is not entrenched. This is not a 4,000-year society."

Though educated in England, he said he was not much the student of one of the great European political intellectuals of the 20th century—the late Sir Isaiah Berlin, whose short book *The Hedgehog and the Fox* (1953) helped frame our conversations for this book. We had a light tussle over my proposal that he was a Hedgehog (a big ideas man), but he took the view that, if anything between the two, he was a Fox (a man of hundreds of practical ideas, not just a few overriding ones).

At the end of the last session I handed him a copy of the book. He seemed surprised and said, "This is for me?" I laughed and said that yes, it was a gift. I also said that as far as I knew, Berlin (who taught at Oxford) was in his thinking about the 'Fox' philosophy as close as anyone to Lee Kuan Yew (who studied at Cambridge). This is evident in a longer book by Berlin that I later mailed to Lee. *Personal Impressions* is a string of short pearls of personality profiles strung together into a 1981 volume starring famous thinkers whom Berlin admired.

Berlin, who died in 1997, was not writing of Lee in these richly woven passages, of course; but as you will see, he might well have been.

Take, for example, this about the austere J.L. Austin, the Oxford philosopher. Berlin wrote: "He was not doctrinaire. He did not hold with programmes.... He treated problems piecemeal as they came, not as part of a systematic reinterpretation."

Or about the famed British historian Richard Pares: "His distaste for philosophy ... developed in distrust of all general ideas. He disliked speculation and preoccupation with questions capable of no clear answers.... Attempts to raise fundamental issues, whether personal or historical, were stopped by a few dry words, with growing impatience and even irritation. He had always detested romantic rhetoric, ostentation, journalism."

Now, whom does that sound like?

Or about his Oxford colleague and political theorist John Petrov Plamenatz, encouraged by his tutor W.G. Maclagan in the realistic tradition of moral philosophy: "He occupied no recognizable position and founded no school.... He did not modify or shape his thought to make it fit into a system, he did not look for a unifying historical or metaphysical structure ... so that those who looked for a system, an entire edifice of thought to attach themselves to, went away dissatisfied...."

Lee always emphasized his ad-hoc pragmatism. I fought him on this point, at best to a draw. But I may have been wrong. In Berlin's terminology, Lee is indeed a Fox, not a Hedgehog. I may have underestimated the overall impact of the tremendous atmospheric pressure of empiricism at Cambridge, where he read law and graduated with double First Class Honours. This successful experience at such a hallowed institution would have left a deep impression on anyone. It might have made me almost religious about what I had learned, made me even unyieldingly Hedgehogian about my British pragmatism.

Fox or not, Lee was a steel icon for what we Americans would label the law and order thing. He was stricter than the sternest father. His insistence on the virtues of discipline, hard work and respect for authority put the filial piety of a nation to the test.

A joke at his expense. And so two dogs are swimming in the waters between Singapore and Borneo—but in opposite directions. They pause halfway to exchange greetings. The dog headed toward Borneo asked the other dog why he's swimming to Singapore. The answer: "Ah, the shopping, the housing, the air conditioning, the health care, the schools. So why are you going to Borneo?" Says the dog from Singapore: "Oh, I just want to bark."

The hurry-up offense of the Lee Kuan Yew ambition to First-World Singapore was competing against the ticking clock of competition and globalization. The rush to build and grow was understandable and the performance exceptional. But it was predicated on a political system that in quieting the news media put enormous pressure on the government and the People's Action Party to monitor corruption and inferior performance. This was the system's Achilles heel. Inevitably some bad stuff had to have been kept from public view. But in time it will come out—and for all anyone knows, there may be a good deal of it.

The system of control Lee clamped on the small island city-state was somewhat suffocating. Arts and literature were slow to develop even as the scientific, mathematical and engineering skills soared to exceed the achievement level of almost all nations. Singapore's per capita income level, greater than even the U.S. and probably Japan, were a testament to the economic success, brilliantly achieved in the flash of a few decades. But there was a downside, a cost, as there is with almost everything. His daughter Wei Ling hints at it in this book in her critique of mere materialism as a measure of exemplary national achievement. But asked about it, her father (who like all of us fathers always knows best) is defensive and dismissive.

Consider those striking (but in my mind silly) opinion polls finding Singaporeans to be the least happy people on the planet (and those in Panama the happiest—can you believe??); or that they are the least emotional of any people (and those in the Philippines the most emotional—well, *that* one can be believed!). We don't have to buy into all that poll baloney to know that material success cannot offer all that we want to be. We in America are particularly well aware that happiness and a truly rounded culture cannot simply be gauged in dollar signs.

Lee was all but blind to that because he was hell-bent to see his country escape from Third World poverty. And that he did. But there was tunnel vision to the route of the canal he burrowed. He felt that if he took his eye off the economic ball, the juggernaut that was Singapore would slow down, lose momentum and slide into reverse. Every day he woke up, he would look for new coal to fire into the engine.

And in the end he got his way. In Singapore politics it usually went Lee's way—and that of his PAP party, which he dominated. I emphasize this because the late Earl Latham, who was chairman of the political science department at Amherst College when I was an undergraduate, always proposed defining politics thusly: "Politics is getting your own way. Nothing more." It is getting your own way as much as you can.

And that rather nicely characterized Singapore politics for decades—Lee Kuan Yew getting his own way. Right, enemies might face jail time if necessary, critics faced costly litigation in the courts, and the mere sight or voice of Lee could scare.

But there was a payoff to the public: Singapore got to the land that Lee had promised—to be a first class First World nation. It was almost a textbook success, except he was the one writing the book, and writing it as he went along, as he'd be the first to admit.

The achievement was not always pretty. Leaving aside the relentless drumbeat of criticism from foreign human rights groups, mostly those in the U.S. (as if the U.S. hasn't its own issues in that regard), it is true Singapore had less "freedom" than classically defined. Yes, it has more money, more stability, more social cohesion, more international clout—but not more freedom to … well … bark.

Lee was well aware of what he was doing. Effective leaders usually do. They will do what they have to do. In classical political philosophy, the "Doctrine of Dirty Hands" postulates that all leaders will have to do things that otherwise would be morally (and probably legally) unacceptable in less authorized hands. Let us note mild-mannered, professorial President Obama—the former lecturer from Harvard Law School—keeps a hit list of possible terrorist targets at his White House desk. And so on around the globe.

Power is not pretty. Whether it comes from the barrel of a gun, from the gavel of a judge, or from the mouth of authority, it is inherently forceful and coercive. People tend not to understand power. Even when used for a good cause, it is not a nice thing.

Lee earlier in the book denies he was a soft authoritarian, as that term of political art goes, on the grounds that his PAP party had put itself before voters and had been repeatedly validated. But without the decades of dazzling economic success, what would have happened? The suspicion is that by and large voters would have been too intimidated to vote otherwise. But we never had to see the worst. Lee delivered. He used power—

absolute and persuasive—effectively. He got the job done that he set out to do.

By fax once I once asked him to offer some self-criticism. He referred me to Catherine Lim. This fine writer, perhaps his most persistently perceptive critic, at the end of a long lecture in the summer of 2012 that contained quite a listing of his alleged errors and foibles, nonetheless was forced to conclude this way:

> "We are indeed in the midst of one of the most exciting times in Singapore's history, a time fraught with paradoxes, perils and promises, brought about a general election [2011] that has been described as a watershed, a sea change, a transformation, not least because it ended the era of Lee Kuan Yew. Mr Lee's legacy is so mixed that at one end of the spectrum of response, there will be adulation, and at the other, undisguised opprobrium and distaste. But whatever the emotions he elicits, whatever the controversies that swirl around him, it will be generally agreed that for a man of his stature and impact, neither the present nor the future holds an equal."

No definitive, measured assessment of the Lee Kuan Yew era is possible right now. History needs to sort through the basic metrics and give them some ranking. Consider the daunting question of the true value of electoral democracy—one citizen, one vote. Is this system a moral imperative? As we have seen, Lee thinks not. Many people admire the U.S. but they also give enormous credit to China, despite its authoritarian system. Is any kind of political system that delivers very good governance and economic development, as did Lee's, a manifest social good? And is a democracy that fails to do that still justifiable, simply because it is a democracy?

The mystery of Lee Kuan Yew and what his successful Singapore represents is not for the simple-minded or those impatient for quick answers. It is profound. But at the end of his story, he stood as the longest serving prime minister in world history. However much we admired his governance policies, we cannot ignore his politics. At the same time, however harsh they were, they worked. He usually knew what he was doing.

He also understood that modernism driven by relentless technological advances forces governments into making major decisions more quickly than is wise. This meant leaders have less freedom of movement in having to bend to the storm of technology. He was surely old-fashioned. At first he instinctively opposed the licensing and building of casinos, and would laugh when he looked back at his hopelessly ineffective antipathy to the dominance of the automobile as the main mode of transportation in cramped Singapore. If he could have had his way, he would have tricked up the city-state's mass transit systems to make movement much easier and made automobile possession even more difficult and expensive than it in fact became.

Another regret came up in 1996 during my first interview with him at the Istana. It concerned the economic and professional advancement of women, which Singapore, in its rush for economic development, went all out to push. The country quickly almost doubled the size of its adult workforce. But there were other consequences, he said:

> "The danger for a traditional society is either they educate their women the way the West has done, which means they become equally well educated, or they do it like the Japanese, where women are not as well educated and jobs for women are temporary. It was a deliberate choice made by the elders of Japan. They studied America but decided to keep women in their traditional roles—as wives, mothers and custodians of the next generation. And [even with that], Japan has been able to catch up with the rest of the world...."

At the time of this interview, Japan's economy was the world's second largest. He continued:

> "We went the way of the West; we knocked down all the barriers and allowed our women to compete. Now we are in very serious difficulties, because our men won't marry their educational equals. It's against traditional culture. We're not Americans, that's the problem.... We have upset age-old traditions too fast, especially the attitudes of mothers."

One of Lee's qualities that a newspaper column or even a book cannot easily capture is his refined manner of enunciation. But it is so content-driven that it does not come across as affected. Over the decades my ear encountered little like it, not even from Tony Blair or John Major, both of whom I have interviewed.

Lee concluded:

> "The basic relationships have been disrupted. If we had taken more time, we would have had fewer problems.... The Japanese are very determined to avoid changing the fundamental relationship within the family. But we opened the floodgates and find ourselves deluged."

The whole point of the 'Giants of Asia' series, of which this was the inaugural volume, was to get behind official veneer. After the book was released in 2010, I received a note from an intimate of his who said he learned things from it even though he had worked with Lee for decades. This was nice to know but I am aware there is much more to his story and that of the other 'Giants of Asia' figures who followed.

You do the best you can with what you are able to work with. It's true that Lee offered me less time than did the three subjects who followed—Malaysia's Mahathir, Thailand's Thaksin and South Korea's Ban Ki-moon, the UN Secretary General. But with Lee, you require less time because he packs so much wallop into each sentence and paragraph. There is little fooling around. The second in the 'Giants' chorus line, Mahathir—so eager to outdo Lee in all things—doubled down on the time commitment for our conversations. Number three was the irrepressible Thaksin, Thailand's prime minister from 2001–06, unceremoniously ejected from elective office by an illegal military/political coup. The feisty and quietly furious billionaire politician was eager to get his side of the story painted on a broad international canvas; he not only signed up for more hours than the good Malaysian doctor but also threw in a long last-minute Skype as, later, did his sister Yingluck, just prior to her triumphant election as Thailand's first lady prime minister.

But perhaps most surprisingly of all, there was Ban Ki-moon, who even while perched on the deeply tricky if worthy cliff of secretary general of the United Nations, graciously proposed more sessions than anyone—on his own down time. This commitment was admirable. The trio of Lee, Mahathir and Thaksin were looking back on their time in the sun. But Ban was still in the hot seat. We met on Saturday mornings or after work for two-hour sessions. Occasionally, with his deeply intuitive wife Soon-Taek at his side, he talked to me in restaurants and a supper club or two to which I had more or less dragged them. By nature cautious and shy, this Korean over-achiever nonetheless sought to reveal as much as he could without tipping over into verbal behavior or revelation unbecoming of the world's top diplomat. He was committed to quality and I admired that but he was no easy interview.

Neither were Mahathir or Thaksin, but out of office they had a few scores they wanted to settle and a clutched handful of secrets to reveal. Dr. Mahathir would let out a ludicrous bombast that I had to try hard to take seriously (without much success). Thaksin would sometimes play the role of the innocent which, of course, was impossible to take seriously. But both, like Ban, were committed to trying to help make the book a serious and useful one for today's readers and, perhaps as well, for future generations.

But as for Lee, let us put it this way: in his manner of his articulation he was more succinct than these three put together. I doubt if any of the above would begrudge my saying this, much less disagree with it. In fact I am not sure any of the three would have consented to these books had Lee not agreed to have gone first. All politics and personalities aside, they greatly respected his achievements and, to some extent, his unique style. They figured that if 'Giants' was good enough for Lee—hardly notorious for being anyone's fool—it was probably good enough for them.

Lee's approach on policy and political issues, especially in semi-retirement, was to get to the point without taking prisoners along the way. But on the personal side, the big revealing book on Lee the person will be tough to do. As articulate as he was about his beloved Singapore, he kept an interior side to himself that perhaps only his late wife—or surviving daughter—ever fully saw. The tough guy tried to hide any human vulnerability and for my part, I tried on these pages to cut through some of the aura. I'd venture a silly joke or a jolting josh here and there, knowing in advance that every move in the reporter's unofficial book of tricks had been tried on him. But I tried anyway. I'd become absurdly confessional (who really cared about my story, right?), chattering on about myself regarding this and that, trying to get him to laugh at me so as to get him to reflect and talk more about himself. But much that lies beneath the glacial smooth surface of this eloquent world figure is yet to be excavated. This book was but a start.

In the short story *Masterson*, Somerset Maugham writes of a certain man he met while on a steamer to Malaysia: "He was a tall, dark fellow with … aloofness of manner…. Men like this are a little restless in the company of others and though in the smoking-room of a ship or at the club they may be talkative and convivial, telling their story with the rest, joking and glad sometimes to narrate their unusual experiences, they seem always to hold something back. They have a life in themselves that they keep apart, and there is a look in their eyes, as it were turned inwards, that informs you that this hidden life is the only one that signifies to them…. They then seem to long for the monotonous solitude of some place of their predilection where they can be once more alone with the reality they have found."

I like to imagine that Maugham—at his literary height in the 1930s—had met Lee in some prior time and place, because that description of Masterson is the man I have met and known, however episodically, over the years. And now, in fact, he is more alone than ever with the reality he helped create: the Singapore of his dreams.

Lee Kuan Yew at the Biltmore Hotel, Los Angeles, 1998, just before he gave a terrific keynote lunchtime speech. To his right is Toshiaki Ogasawara, publisher and chair of the *Japan Times*; to his left, Jack Stark, president of Claremont-McKenna College. Just a few hours before, police received a death threat on his life, hence the presence of a U.S. secret service agent (back row). Lee, though, was as cool as a chilled cucumber.

I was sitting across from him when one of three student aides, from UCLA, came up to me and asked if the senior minister would consent to a quick picture. I told Alice (center) I doubted it but she was persistent. LKY noticed the action and gave me a look. Though fully expecting to be coldly rebuffed, I communicated the request. Without hesitating he said, "Sure, but I have one favor to ask." What's that? "Send me a copy." I said he had a deal. And I did.

Shandray, Alice and Leila then swung around the rope and moved toward Lee. The agent quickly put his body in the way (the girls clearly were 'dangerous' but also clearly not packing!) and Lee intervened to say, "No, it's okay. Let them in." Then they moved behind him quickly, and we get this charming snapshot. (Photo courtesy of Tom Plate)

A Foreign Affair

As the international reputation of Singapore grew, so did the complexity of its foreign policy. This did not happen all at once.

Return to 1996, my first meeting with Lee Kuan Yew: This was more than a dozen years prior to the intense conversations in 2009 that comprise this book. This took place in his spacious but plain, no-nonsense office in Istana, the government house. And this was six years after the founder of modern Singapore had handed the job of prime minister over to his chosen successor, thus marking the end of his 31-year run in office—the longest of any PM in recorded political history.

But if he was technically out of power, he was anything but out of influence; and even by 1996 his reputation and status were almost legendary, in many parts of Asia at least. But not in the West, and certainly not in U.S. media circles: The problem was that almost all that any editor or journalist knew of Singapore was its apparent harshness, as related to them in invariably critical reports from the human-rights community, and in portraits of Lee based on little more than relentlessly recycled caricatures, not actual on-scene reporting, much less personal meetings.

The U.S. problem, besides ignorance, was that the 'Sings' just did not do things the American way, and so LKY (as he'd sign personal notes) was prone to depiction as no more than an authoritarian ogre. It was as if the 'caning and chewing gum' imagery was permanently stuck onto the face of Singapore in perpetuity, with Lee serving as a far-away whipping boy for human-rights groups and know-it-all columnists, especially the late William Safire of the *New York Times*. In October 1996, "More Homeowners Than Hardliners"—my first column on Singapore in the *Los Angeles Times*—appeared in an effort to offer some balance. In obvious response, Bill countered with a nasty "The Little Hitler of Southeast Asia".

Safire, ordinarily an outstanding columnist, had an advantage over me in writing about Lee and his Singapore. It is easier to hammer stereotypes when you're writing about a country which (at that point) you had never visited and about a man you had never met. In this negligent sense, Safire really did reflect the Western media. He really didn't know what he was writing about but went ahead and wrote it anyway. In truth, Lee, though publicly—but also sincerely—dismissive of the West's media, was also immensely frustrated by his city-state's bad press, and worked patiently and relentlessly to reach out to the media with a different Singapore story.

In fact, this tough-minded, blunt-talking, almost scarily articulate Hakka-Chinese politician did have a splendid, almost heroic story to tell. Pushed out by insecure sultans and potentates to the north in Malaysia who feared the ambitions of the cunning, fast-footed Lee, Singapore was cast out to sink or swim on its own. But could it do it all alone? While it was so vulnerably small, history did offer encouraging precedents. There were such glorious city-states of yore—Rome, Athens and Carthage—and contemporary ones, such as Monaco and Qatar. To make Singapore into what it is today was an immense achievement—but it was not without precedent. To make Singapore into what it is today was an immense achievement—but it was not without precedent. Surely, the country's scholars and nerds were well aware that they had a good chance of success because, after all, it more or less had been done before.

But Venice's way could not be Singapore's way and, to my mind at least, what stood out as much as how Singapore achieved its high standard of living was its high standard of thinking. In spending so good time with Lee and his top people here and there over two decades, I began to think that in addition to having a GDP (gross domestic product) index to gauge national achievement, maybe we could use one called something like NIQ—National Intelligence Quotient. If the island state ranked at only 30-something (because so tiny) on the world GDP, it might be right up there near number one with NIQ.

But if sheer intellect was its strong suit, modesty was not, and as Singapore moved to the head of the Southeast Asian class—and sometimes bragged about it—the region's lesser 'students' became jealous. What to do? How to hide from your peers that you're brilliant? The answer it came up with was a regional diplomacy in equal conjunction with a globalized strategy. In the immediate Southeast Asia arena, Lee and his tight coterie conspired to compliment the national and commercial interests of neighbors, so fearful were they of being left out in the cold, while at the same time luring major Western and Japanese multinationals to nest and invest in a country increasingly stable, English-speaking and, most of all, well-educated.

The key geopolitical decision was an early one: agreeing to link arms, soon after declaring nationhood, with Indonesia, Malaysia, the Philippines and Thailand to create out of nothing ASEAN (Association of Southeast Asian Nations). Today, this economic and political conglomerate of states, now ten-members strong, adds up to the world's seventh largest economy. Truth be told, though, Singapore was neither the first to join nor, originally, the happiest about the idea. It feared being overwhelmed and/or undervalued by nations so much larger and, in some cases, so Islamic. But Lee and his cabinet came to accept that Singapore would have no comfortable future unless it played nicely with neighbors. Staying aloof was a theoretical thought, but it was not a practical option. Still, as one well-known Asia diplomat told me: "Singapore more or less jumped in at the last minute."

But jump in it did, with the pluses outweighing the negatives, but not drowning. Today most ASEAN members have the worry of rather significant economic and territorial issues with giant China. But not Singapore, which feels it has other fish to fry and endeavors to cultivate practical positivity with Beijing as well as Washington. Only two-track diplomacy makes sense. And so, as we see just recently, it jumped onto the fast-moving train of China's Asian Infrastructure Investment Bank, despite the initially near-hysterical opposition of Washington to Beijing's idea.

Not surprisingly, sometimes one hears the complaint that the city-state all too cynically plays both sides of the street. But in truth the dexterous Singapore really doesn't care to respond to the obvious. If it's ideological in any sense of the word at all, it's in the relentlessness of its pragmatism. In the initial years of nationhood, for instance, the young prime minister installed a system of compulsory national service and induced experts from Israel—of all places—to organize the training. This was done in the general region of a largely Islamic neighborhood. Another example: Singapore conducts joint military exercises not only with China, but with Taiwan as well—all the while somehow avoiding getting trapped in their poisonous reunification psychodrama. Now, this cannot be so easy a trick.

China remains more on Singapore's mind than anything. Going back to that first interview meeting in 1996, Lee impressed on me the urgent and complex question of the Beijing-Washington bilateral relationship. No one issue was more important, he said; it was the core geopolitical question of the first half of the 21st century.

Derwin Pereira, a former key journalist with *The Straits Times* who heads a Singapore-based political consultancy, explained in an email to me: "Mr Lee Kuan Yew's greatest diplomatic achievement

270 | TOM PLATE

was to serve as an interlocutor between America and China. He was sufficiently Chinese to know how the Sinic mind worked, and he was sufficiently Western to know how the American mind worked. What is extraordinary is that the leaders of both great powers paid him so much attention since he was but from a city-state."

With more than a bit of flair, LKY tripped around the world far more than any Southeast Asian leader of his generation and was listened to with far more attentiveness than the geopolitical weight his country merited. This was due to two factors. One was the impressive economic and technological growth that all decent leaders wanted to figure out how to emulate. The other was his remarkable understanding of difficult world issues and the intellectual crispness and bracing clarity of his presentations. How many leader-speeches have we all heard that sound more or less like all the other boring ones we have heard? Not Lee's: He was more for straight talking than dodging. His speeches radiated architectural design as well as substance.

Globetrotting diplomat Tommy Koh, who served as Singapore's ambassador to the United Nations and as ambassador to the U.S., explains: "Mr Lee travelled extensively on behalf of Singapore. He befriended and earned the respect of many foreign leaders, in government, business and academia. He had an impressive global network. For example, he was respected by Chinese leader Deng Xiaoping, German leader Helmut Schmidt, French leader Jacques Chirac and Japanese leader Kiichi Miyazawa. He knew and was respected by every American president, from

Lyndon Johnson to Barack Obama. Two of America's thought leaders, Dr Henry Kissinger and Dr George Shultz, are among his many admirers."

No doubt his particular history with Deng Xiaoping helps explain the esteem with which his Singapore is held in China even today. This goes back to the now-legendary tour through Southeast Asia by then Senior Vice-Premier Deng in 1978. Singapore was the final stop, and Lee and his team regaled the future communist emperor of China with the sights and sounds of a bustling Singapore that had the virtue, in contrast to China, of an economic system that hadn't kept all its Chinese citizens in hopeless poverty. This Deng noticed fully, believed Lee, happy to have played a role, and from that point forward seeking to position himself as something of a back seat driver for the little big man steering China onto the freeway of economic reform.

It was from Lee—and from others, of course, not to mention from his own common sense—that Deng came to accept the very large and initially largely unnerving idea that only major doses of entrepreneurial capitalism could save Communist China from the self-destruction of an economically anorexic ideology. As Lee had put it to me in the summer of 2009: "The Chinese know that I have helped them in the past. The ideas that Deng Xiaoping formed, if he had not come here and seen the multinationals in Singapore producing wealth for us, training our people so as a result we were able to build a prosperous society, then he might never have opened [China] up." In addition, Lee would proudly point to Chinese Premier Zhu Rongji's 1990 visit for a crash course on public housing and health insurance programs. And there were other examples of influence.

Lee viewed Deng as the greatest leader he had personally met. During Lee's premiership, some had wondered why capitalist Singapore (which supported America's intervention in Vietnam against communist Hanoi) was trying so hard to help communist China. Again, this was his way: Ever practical, he argued that China would not remain poor forever and Singapore could reap considerable benefits if the Chinese viewed it as a helper.

At the same time street-smart diplomacy kept Singapore balanced atop the tightrope of pleasing the U.S. as well. Today, the U.S. Navy docks ships and the U.S. Air Force lands jet fighters on Singapore territory as U.S. military personnel are quietly housed at the island-state's far northern end.

Singapore, whose population is little more than half of Tokyo's, will tend to view itself as a small (but clever) animal trying to stay out of harm's way in a jungle of elephants. Like the fox that knows so many different ways to survive and thrive, it will use almost any method, tender a nation almost any insincere compliment, and slip and slide and dodge in the dead of night to avoid having to make a choice when not choosing any works best for Singapore.

Cheong Yip Seng, for years the editor-in-chief of Singapore's *The Straits Times* newspaper, and author of the acclaimed *OB Markers: My Straits Times Story*, a gripping inside look at the media system during the LKY years, explains: "Geography is destiny, it is said. Singapore is a tiny island in what was for many years since independence a very hostile environment. Who is to guarantee the environment will remain stable as it is now? How, for instance, will the U.S.-China relationship develop? So Singapore has to make as many friends as possible, stay non-aligned, and resist being treaty allies so it has maximum room to maneuver. Singapore needs a stable environment to maximize its chances of growth. Without growth, instability sets in, and its vulnerability increases, threatening its territorial integrity."

And it was in this dance-and-dodge-as-fast-as-you-can spirit that the subject of Japan would pop up on LKY's geopolitical radar even as he had seemed preoccupied with the Sino-U.S. relationship. In fact, in almost every conversation with him I would hear some version of his admonition never to count Japan out of the Asian equation. Singapore's Derwin Pereira explains: "In spite of his terrible experience of the Japanese occupation of Singapore, Mr Lee was an admirer of the Japanese industrial ethic and quest for discipline and perfection at work. The Japanese desire to learn from best practices elsewhere, including the United States, is a trait that he imported into Singapore."

In interviews with me he was emphatic, almost emotional, about his admiration of things Japanese, especially the historic tendency to elide into one molten-iron mentality in the face of severe crisis. He also came to appreciate the understandable reluctance to fast-track employment equality for women (as Singapore had, a decision about which Lee had mixed feelings), and worried why their leaders were not always as top-notch as Yasuhiro Nakasone or Kiichi Miyazawa.

Lee's breadth of cultural viewpoint always struck me as helpful and wise. It seemed to arise out of an intellectual cosmopolitanism that went far beyond what one would expect of the leader of such a tiny country. But perhaps even in geopolitics, size isn't always everything. Singapore, after all, evolved into one of the world's most talked about and (in some quarters, at least) admired of nations in the course of the last half of the 20th century. But it is such the shivering shrimp in the vast boiling seas of Asia—with a population less than Hong Kong's, a fourth of Australia's, barely a tenth of South Korea's; and a land mass half that of Los Angeles and two-thirds that of Hong Kong.

Singapore's core firepower was always its brainpower, and until his recent death, it had one of modern history's true geopolitical brainiacs to show off to everyone. And what a fine thing that was. But now he is gone—to Singapore, and to the rest of us. I, for one, will miss his counsel greatly.

"Mr Lee Kuan Yew will go down in history as one of the most influential leaders of the 20th century," flatly states Dean Kishore Mahbubani of the Lee Kuan Yew School of Public Policy and author of *The Great Convergence.*

A serious exaggeration? Only history can decide. But I have found that this dean is usually right—and in this case, certainly, I agree with him.

Works Consulted

Cheong, Yip Seng. *OB Markers: My Straits Times Story.* Straits Times Press: Singapore, 2012.

Datta-Ray, Sunanda K. *Looking East to Look West.* ISEAS Publishing: Institute of Southeast Asian Studies, Singapore, 2009.

Han Fook Kwang, et al. *Lee Kuan Yew, The Man and His Ideas.* Times Editions: Singapore, 1998.

Lai, Ah Eng, ed. *Beyond Rituals and Riots, Ethnic Pluralism and Social Cohesion in Singapore.* Eastern Universities Press: Singapore, 2004.

Lee, Kuan Yew. *The Singapore Story.* Simon & Schuster: New York, 1998.

_____. *From Third World to First, The Singapore Story: 1965–2000.* HarperCollins: New York, 2000.

Minchin, James. *No Man Is an Island: A Study of Singapore's Lee Kuan Yew.* Allen & Unwin: Australia, 1986

Schuman, Michael. *The Miracle: The Epic Story of Asia's Quest for Wealth.* HarperCollins: New York, 2009.

Tan, Wee Kiat, et al. *Gardens of the Istana.* National Parks Board: Singapore, 2003, 2008.

Trocki, Carl A. *Singapore: Wealth, Power and the Culture of Control.* Routledge: New York, 2006.

Yap, Sonny, et al. *Men In White: The Untold Story of Singapore's Ruling Party.* Singapore Press Holdings/Marshall Cavendish Editions: Singapore, 2009.

Thanking those who helped make this book possible

Minister Mentor Lee Kuan Yew, Singapore's founder and subject of this book, never once asked to review the manuscript, of course, but he did ask to look over all direct quotes for accuracy, content and style. I happily agreed, and sincerely appreciated his effort to improve accuracy and articulation, as well as his patient and precise responses to the emails over these past months, not to mention the exclusive hours on 27 and 28 July, 2009 at the Istana, and his interviews with me over the years.

Chris Newson, the forward-looking general manager and publisher of Marshall Cavendish, never stopped thinking about how to make a bit of history with this book; I liked that! **Violet Phoon,** former managing editor of Marshall Cavendish, and the late **Theron Raines,** of Raines & Raines, my career-long literary agent, were invaluable, absolutely essential, thoroughly professional, relentlessly demanding and mutually incomparable. **My Lu,** Fletcher School of Law and Diplomacy '09, was the book's senior researcher and contributed significantly to it in a number of ways, as she has to many of my efforts over the years.

And **Lee Mei Lin,** senior editor of Marshall Cavendish, kept my feet to the flames of proper usage, grammar and taste; and I do indeed thank her.

David Armstrong, the well-known career journalist and chief editor at newspapers from Sydney to Hong Kong, read an early draft and made valuable suggestions. **Professor Bin Wong,** UCLA's pre-eminent Chinese historian and Director of the UCLA Asia Institute, kindly read and commented on the original manuscript. His views were deeply thoughtful. Even so, neither he nor David Armstrong are responsible for its contents in any way, except to the extent that parts of it may be excellent.

Reading and improving earlier drafts were **Nicole Riggs,** a former UCLA student, former column-checker and graduate of the Woodrow Wilson School of Public and International Affairs at Princeton University, my own alma mater; and **Anya Zabolotnaya,** a former UCLA course assistant, working actress (Anya Benton) and column-editor at the Pacific Perspectives Media Center. Finally, appreciation for wise input go to **D. Katharine Lee** of the Georgetown University School of Medicine in Washington, DC.

About the Author

TOM PLATE, author of the ongoing 'Giants of Asia' series, is an American journalist with an international career at media institutions from London to Los Angeles. Born in New York, he completed his studies at Amherst College and Princeton University's Woodrow Wilson School of Public and International Affairs, where he earned his master's degree in public and international affairs. His syndicated columns focusing on Asia and America, begun in 1996, have run in major newspapers in Asia and America.

He has received awards from the American Society of Newspaper Editors, the California Newspaper Publishers Association and the Greater Los Angeles Press Club. When he was Editor of Editorial Pages of the *Los Angeles Times*, the newspaper garnered the Pulitzer Prize for its coverage of the Los Angeles riots.

From 1994 to 2008, he taught in the communication and policy studies programs at the University of California, Los Angeles. He has been a Media Fellow at Stanford University and a fellow in Tokyo at the Japanese Foreign Press Center's annual Asia-Pacific

Media Conference. He is currently Distinguished Scholar of Asian and Pacific Studies at Loyola Marymount University, Los Angeles, as well as a former Visiting Professor at United Arab Emirates University in Al Ain, UAE.

He was the founder of the non-profit Asia Pacific Media Network (APMN), whose webpage resurfaced as *Asia Media International* at Loyola Marymount University in Los Angeles (lmu.edu/asiamedia). He also founded the Pacific Perspectives Media Center in Beverly Hills, California, a non-profit op-ed service.

On the West Coast, he is a board member of the Pacific Century Institute and a Senior Fellow at the USC Center for the Digital Future; on the East Coast he is a long-standing member of the Princeton Club of New York and the Phi Beta Kappa Society. For years he was a participant at the retreats of the World Economic Forum in Davos, Switzerland.

Professor Plate is the author of twelve books, including the bestsellers *Confessions of an American Media Man* (2007), *Conversations with Lee Kuan Yew* (2010), *Conversations with Mahathir Mohamad* (2011), *Conversations with Thaksin* (2011) and *Conversations with Ban Ki-moon* (2012). His other works include *In the Middle of the Future* (2013), *In the Middle of China's Future* (2014) and *The Fine Art of the Political Interview* (2015), all published by Marshall Cavendish Editions. Under a pseudonym, he is the author of the novel *The Only Way to Go*. He resides in Beverly Hills with his wife Andrea, a licensed clinical social worker, and their three cats: Rafael, Rufianne and Leonardo.

Other books in the 'Giants of Asia' series

Conversations with Ban Ki-moon
What the United Nations Is Really Like:
The View From the Top

ISBN: 978 981 4302 04 3
240 pp

Conversations with Thaksin
From Exile to Deliverance: Thailand's
Populist Tycoon Tells His Story

ISBN: 978 981 4328 68 5
252 pp

Conversations with Mahathir Mohamad
Doctor M: Operation Malaysia

ISBN: 978 981 4276 63 4
248 pp